MW01010517

THE MIND

ITS PROJECTIONS
AND MULTIPLE FACETS

YOGI BHAJAN, PhD

WITH GURUCHARAN SINGH KHALSA, PhD

Kundalini Research Institute
Training • Publishing • Research • Resources

© 1998 Kundalini Research Institute
Published by the Kundalini Research Institute
PO Box 1819, Santa Cruz, NM 87567
www.kundaliniresearchinstitute.org

ISBN 978-0-9639991-6-0

DESIGN & LAYOUT
Guru Raj Kaur Khalsa

COVER DESIGN
Sopurkh Singh Khalsa

GRAPHICS
Jim Weidenhamer

ILLUSTRATIONS
Shabad Kaur Khalsa

FRONT COVER PHOTOGRAPH
Soorya Kaur Khalsa

BACK COVER PHOTOGRAPH
Sat Kartar Kaur Khalsa

TRANSCRIPTIONIST
Tej Kaur Khalsa

VIDEO TAPES
Golden Temple Enterprises

PRINTER
Sheridan Books

About Yogi Bhajan

YOGI BHAJAN, PhD, taught from 1969 to 2004 in every part of the globe. An incomparable teacher, Yogi Bhajan set the standard as an exceptional lecturer and a unique and powerful teacher of teachers. He earned his reputation as a wise and trusted counselor and mentor while teaching the keys to meditation, the mind, health, healing, relationships, and spirituality.

Born in 1929, Yogi Bhajan mastered Kundalini Yoga and Meditation at the age of 16. He later became the Mahan Tantric (Master of White Tantric Yoga). He earned his Masters Degree in Economics (1952) and his doctorate in the Psychology of Communication (1980). The author of more than 30 books, Yogi Bhajan's teachings are available in more than 200 other books and videos. They are a treasury of wisdom and inspiration. His teachings were precise and practical yet universal, appealing to everyone, regardless of creed, race, country, caste, or profession.

Yogi Bhajan was given the unique ministerial position of Siri Singh Sahib of Sikh Dharma of the Western Hemisphere (Chief Religious and Administrative Authority). He inspired both Sikhs and non-Sikhs to live to the highest standards of spirituality, commitment, and compassion. He was the recipient of many awards and proclamations for his work to promote peace, inter-religious cooperation, conscious business enterprises and healthy lifestyles.

To reach and uplift every person, Yogi Bhajan established the 3HO Foundation (Healthy, Happy, Holy Organization) in the United States in 1969. The 3HO Foundation belongs to the United Nations group of Non-Government Organizations and is a global community that promotes healthy, conscious lifestyles in countries around the world. The 3HO legacy lives on and grows with the same spirit of joy, sharing, acceptance, vitality and contribution that he gave it.

Everything he shared, even the most esoteric teachings, were to further the simple goal of achieving happiness and spiritual fulfillment so that each one of us could live a life of excellence. A visionary, a teacher, an inspiration and a leader to millions of people, he established a legacy that continues to serve humanity.

About Gurucharan Singh Khalsa

GURUCHARAN SINGH KHALSA, PhD, is an expert in Kundalini Yoga as taught by Yogi Bhajan, and has been his student and primary interpreter and compiler of his teachings since 1969. Dr. Khalsa combines Western scientific training with Eastern traditions to develop practical approaches to personal growth and fulfillment. His first degrees and graduate studies were from Harvey Mudd College and Claremont Graduate School. His major emphasis was in mathematics, with a broad training in physics, chemistry, engineering and a minor in psychology. Later Dr. Khalsa earned both an M.Ed. at Boston University and a Ph.D. in psychology with an emphasis on research in meditation and clinical counseling. He has a keen understanding of Humanology, the psychology of personal excellence developed by Yogi Bhajan, and has used it in clinical practice for three decades as well as developed trainings in Humanology for therapists and healers.

As president of Khalsa Consultants, Inc., he consulted with many businesses and developed seminars and executive coaching to optimize leadership, stress resilience, creativity and conscious communication in teams. He co-authored *Breathwalk* with Yogi Bhajan and co-edited *The Psychospiritual Clinician's Handbook*. In addition, he has contributed original research on the effects and use of Kundalini Yoga and meditation.

Dr. Khalsa is currently the Director of Training for the Kundalini Research Institute (KRI) which he co-founded in 1971. He leads the development of international training programs for teachers in Kundalini Yoga and the research and applications of meditative and yoga techniques to help people deal with happiness, stress, diabesity (diabetes and obesity), positive lifestyles and emotional vitality. He is an expert in Kundalini Yoga, Humanology, and awakening human potential and intuition. He instructed in yoga and wellness psychology at the Massachusetts Institute of Technology for over 15 years and established wellness programs in universities and clinics.

He is committed to sharing the essence of the teachings of Yogi Bhajan to create fulfillment for each individual in spirit, vitality, life purpose and robust communities of consciousness and values.

He is a Mukhia Singh Sahib—a minister—in Sikh Dharma and an active member of the Khalsa Council that serves all of Sikh Dharma.

Acknowledgements

Gratitude and appreciation go to the many people who worked to produce this book. The editors, publisher, designer, and assistants were all dedicated to producing a useful and accurate product. Special thanks go to Gurucharan Kaur Khalsa who brought each chapter to full birth, to Shakti Parwha Kaur Khalsa who edited even parts of words, to Sat Kirpal Kaur Khalsa, Ph.D., for her dual role as both editor and project coordinator for KRI, to Pranpati Singh (John Ricker) for his proofreading and indexing, and to the artistic help of Guru Prakash Singh. Gratitude also goes to our administrative staff support, Mehtab Singh and Dharam Singh, who were constantly helpful.

Always consult your physician before beginning this or any other exercise program. Nothing in this book is to be construed as medical advice. The benefits attributed to the practice of Kundalini Yoga come from the centuries-old yogic tradition. Results will vary with individuals.

Contents

DIAGRAMS & TABLES

Foreword

Talks, Teachings, and Technology of Mind
for the Aquarian Age

I met Yogi Bhajan on a sweltering, smoggy day in southern California. I went expecting a lecture and a meditation. He was speaking at the college I had attended. Instead he gave a talk. He spoke heart to heart. Each word was simple, direct, and planted roots in my depths. He didn't preach nor did he present an argument. He talked in a way that let me see through his eyes. See myself with a new attitude and altitude.

He taught whoever came. He taught wisdom and techniques that were sacred and had been secret for ages. He initiated no one and challenged each of us to take responsibility and initiate our selves. He talked with passion and precision about the fundamentals of living with excellence, grace, and value. With each sentence I knew he was delivering a teaching and that it was not about his personality, nor his national origin, nor personal recognition. It was about awareness and the teachings.

He translated great ideas and abstract insights into everyman's language. Like all great masters and teachers his words touched the unknown potential in each of us. I trusted his blunt directness and his alert sensitivity immediately.

This book tries to capture just a little of that wisdom. Each lecture is really a talk. A heart-to-heart conversation that passes on a vision and an experience. If you read these carefully they will leave you with a little more of your self, with a little wider vision of who you are and how you can be happy in your life.

Before I learned from him, I was told meditations were all the same and that they consist of sitting and making the mind calm. As you will discover in this small volume, it is more accurate to think of meditation as having at least two major components. One is the general training of the attention and ways to hold your awareness. This is like aerobics in physical exercise. It is a general toning for the body and mind. It helps all your functions gradually and systemically. Second, there are specific targeted techniques that focus on some Aspect or Projection of the mind or body. These are like training for specific events in sports. Some muscles need to be strengthened to match the challenge of a particular event. These can also bring the effects of the first component, but not necessarily. They are targeted, faster, and give the practitioner a more detailed map of each area of the mind, or in sports each group of muscles.

No one has given such a complete introduction to both parts of the meditative art and science as Yogi Bhajan has. The techniques he gives us here are the foundation for a practical psychology. He calls that psychology and its tools "Humanology." It is about the entire human being and its capacity for excellence in action, richness in perception, clarity in values, and depth in character and consciousness.

In each talk Yogi Bhajan blends three elements to make a unique and tasty dish. First, insights, humor, and stories that connect us to our daily experiences. How do we communicate? How do we approach our goals at work, at home, and within our self? Second, the philosophy and concepts that map out our relationship to the mind, our self, the ego, and the universe. Abstract but essential ideas that he makes tangible and useful. Third, a toolbox of techniques straight out of the missing owner's manual for the human mind. Unlike many people who talk about grand ideas and leave us wondering what to do, he provides the missing links, the technology of the mind and spirit to act and excel in each area. That consistent focus on practical values, actions, and techniques is his special signature.

All that Yogi Bhajan shares in Humanology is a timely answer to the questions raised by the great transition of our time. He has frequently referred to this shift toward globalization and increased sensitivity as the change to the Aquarian Age. He has said that all of humanity is going through a shift that is mental, as well as social and economic. Our minds are waking up to more sensations and thoughts both consciously and subconsciously. As we go through this expansion, many of us sense it with confusion, subliminal anxiety, fear, and fantasy. In this new psychology he has given us a way we can locate our own inner compass and know the direction and manner by which we can participate and contribute to the world in this new age.

In one of Yogi Bhajan's talks someone asked him, "Are there any guidelines to help us understand this shift to the Aquarian Age? How will the consciousness of our children change? What should we expect?" Yogi Bhajan said that the transition to the new Age is complete in AD 2012. Everything will be different. Then he gave these principles to help us live well during this new time:

Five Guidelines for the Aquarian Age

1 *Recognize that the other person is you.*

2 *There is a way through every block.*

3 *When time is on you, start, and the pressure will be off.*

4 *Understand through compassion or you will misunderstand the times.*

5 *Vibrate the Cosmos. The Cosmos will clear the path.*

The material in this book will be of interest to anyone who wants to raise their standards as a human being; who wants to excel and enjoy each moment of life; who wants to understand deeply the structure and function of the mind; and anyone who wants to learn techniques to apply for healing, counseling, and helping people live a little better, a little lighter, and a little more radiantly every day. Any mistakes or problems in this book are entirely my own as a compiler and student. May you forgive them and may Guru Ram Das offset them.

My unbounded gratitude goes to Yogi Bhajan for this opportunity and for sharing such a legacy with the world. I have had the good fortune and blessing to study under his relentless hammer for three decades. In all these years, in thousands of circumstances, serving millions of people, he has always been kind, compassionate, wise, graceful, and effective. Not once have I seen him falter nor hesitate to carry the heaviest responsibility and burden. He is the living proof of the potential and reality of the techniques and consciousness he has taught.

Gurucharan Singh Khalsa, Ph.D.
Khalsa Consultants, Inc.
Wellesley, Massachusetts
November 5, 1997

How to
Use This Book

THIS BOOK IS NOT AN INTRODUCTION TO MEDITATION, NOR A YOGA book. It is not pure philosophy either. It is a book about the structure of the mind and what you can do to direct, develop, and apply it. It will tell you how to know and understand the mind so it becomes your ally and not your problem, your servant and not your master. It will teach you how you can increase your skills and expand your sensitivity. It will give you practical techniques to apply to the way you think, how you make choices, your values, relationships, and how you maintain balance in your life. It also provides the cornerstone for the foundation of an applied psychology of awareness, Humanology, to achieve optimal human performance.

This book is a collection of eleven talks given over a period of a decade. They are followed by a final overview chapter that synthesizes the Aspects and Projections of the mind into a practical map. This map of the mind is followed by a chapter, which gives you both a guide to meditation, and meditation techniques you can use to create change.

A good place to start is to look over the large diagram inserted at the end of this book. It summarizes all the parts of the mind and their relationships. Then go through the lectures. Gradually the nature and functions of the parts of the mind will become clear to you. As you go through the Meditation Guide, you can refer to the diagram to visualize the relationships between all the parts.

You can browse by reading the talks in any order you want. There is a logical order to the chapters, but each talk stands on its own as well.

The first talk, "Establish Your Relationship," looks at the characteristics of the mind and the need for meditation. The second talk, "Win the Game of Life," deals with how the mind projects a thought and processes it.

Third is "Choose Your Altitude," which explores our choice about the quality and level of our lives. It explains qualities inherent in the nature of a human being. The fourth talk, "Balance The Elements," explains the subtle elements that compose us and shows you how the qualities of the mind reveal themselves in the simplest of our habits and projections. The fifth talk, "Eliminate Mental Intrigues," is a powerful exposition of how we entangle the normal functions of the Negative, Positive, and Neutral Minds to create dramas and problems for ourselves.

The sixth talk, "Look Through the Mind's Window," shows you how we inflate and deflate ourselves. The seventh talk, "Speak With Committed Language," introduces the relationship between your word, your creative power, and your consciousness. Some ways of speaking enhance your life and your mind. Other ways of speaking disconnect your life and mind, and put them at odds. This creates many tragedies which we can avoid. The eighth, "Enrich Your Mind," discusses how to enrich yourself, the need for vastness, and the relationship to a teacher. The ninth, "Select Your Path," examines the choice to live spiritually or neurotically. It discusses our misconceptions about following a spiritual path and how to deal with our emotional patterns. The tenth talk, "Recognize Your Reality," discusses why we do a personal practice, and how our mind and ego challenge our efforts to establish a consistent discipline of awareness. The final talk, "Live Consciously Conscious," brings all these ideas together with a focus on conscious living and what that means to us.

The material that is the densest with new terms and concepts is the twelfth chapter, "Master the 81 Facets." You will do best to look at the diagrams in this chapter and the one at the end of the book as you go through this written material. They act like a road map to an otherwise complicated territory. This chapter gives you a concentrated tour of the nature, concepts, and structure of the mind. It traces how each functional part of the mind is generated. It defines the nature of the nine Aspects, 27 Controlling Projections, and 81 Facets.

The "Meditation Guide" is the last chapter of the book. It is a rich resource of meditation techniques to adjust many parts of the mind that create patterns in your emotions and behavior. It is unique. It can be browsed or read through. If you have never meditated and want to know how to start, be sure to read the brief section at the beginning of the Meditation Guide called "First Steps: Meditation for Absolute Beginners."

This "Meditation Guide" describes 42 meditations and organizes them in relation to the parts of your mind. If you look at the diagram at the back of this book you will see nine Aspects. There is a meditation to strengthen or refine each of these Aspects. This is called a Core Alignment Meditation. The goal of each Core Alignment Meditation is to give you the flexibility to use all nine Aspects of your mind to serve your core purpose.

Under each Aspect you will find three Projections. They are like three legs of a stool that support the different qualities of an Aspect. In the "Meditation Guide" you will find a technique to strengthen or balance each of the 27 Projections. This is called a Synchronization Meditation. Its purpose is to synchronize the Projections in a balanced way, to support the actions of the Aspect related to that Projection.

By reading the descriptions of the Aspects and Projections, you can identify the parts that most closely reflect you. Then use the appropriate meditation to develop, balance, or refine their functions. This is a practical approach to training the mind. It is an introduction to the fundamentals of Humanology.

In Kundalini Yoga and Humanology, as each concept and principle is explored, you are given a technique as a way to test it and master it within your self. This is one of the characteristics of Humanology as founded by Yogi Bhajan. It is an applied psychology of experience. It is important to know a truth, and to have an understanding. It is more important to develop the capacity to live that truth and to act with wisdom.

All together these chapters sketch the nature and challenge of the mind. You may read the talks many times for ongoing inspiration and understanding. Each time you read them new points will stand out, and you will gain a deeper understanding and ability to apply these insights. As you apply them, you will discover a new relationship to your mind. Your mind will become your most powerful friend.

1 Establish Your Relationship

I want to talk to you about your most important companion and its structure, the mind. Every human being who wants to excel and to develop the character and caliber that upholds the values of the soul needs a direct, fundamental relationship to the mind. You must have a basic practical understanding of the mind's conception, properties, Aspects, Projections, and 81 Facets. This is the minimum requirement to develop human sensitivity. So prepare yourself for an intense study. Not an intellectual debate, but an intelligent confrontation with your own experience.

Yogi Bhajan began his direct, personal talks when he first set foot in the United States in 1969. All through the years he emphasized the critical need to know your own mind, to identify its functions, capacities, and projections, and to have a relationship to it. This talk initiates this newest collection that is the basis for a complete approach, study, and psychology of the mind for human excellence.

1

I WANT TO TALK TO YOU ABOUT YOUR MOST IMPORTANT COMPANION and its structure, the mind. Every human being who wants to excel and to develop the character and caliber that upholds the values of the soul, needs a direct, fundamental relationship to the mind. You must have a basic practical understanding of the mind's conception, properties, Aspects, Projections, and 81 Facets. This is the minimum requirement to develop human sensitivity. So prepare yourself for an intense study. Not an intellectual debate, but an intelligent confrontation with your own experience. Why do we need to do this? Guru Nanak told us:

ਮਨਿ ਜੀਤੈ ਜਗੁ ਜੀਤੁ ॥

Man jeetai jag jeet
-Guru Nanak, *Siri Guru Granth Sahib*, page 6 (28th *pauree* of *Japji Sahib)*
By conquering your mind, you can conquer the world.

If we can master the use and command of the mind, we can enjoy this world and live truthfully, gracefully, and prosperously.

Let me give you some opening statements. They are truths to invite you and provoke you in this study:

- Mind is your best friend and your worst enemy.
- There is nothing without mind, and there is nothing with mind.
- Whosoever controls the mind controls the entire psyche of the universe.
- For all your troubles, your own mind is responsible. For your successes, your mind is doing it.
- Mind has an essential faculty to be faster than time and space. As such, it is so dangerous that you can do things that are delusional, imaginative, and unintentional. And equally, it is so beneficial that you can create things that can be miracles.

- The faculty of mind gives you the total facility to express the godliness in you. Mind is a faculty to understand the entire creativity of God.
- Mind is given to you for you.
- If there is no relationship between you and your mind, then there is no guidance between you and your mind. If there is no consolidated guidance between you and your mind, then your life will be nothing but a disaster for you, for your children, and for your generation to follow.
- Mind is the faculty that can deliver the speed and power of God, and it can ruin mankind in its own web of imagination, ego, and desire. Mind is a faculty which, when applied through the ego, only ruins a human being and never lets him grow to be better than a mere animal under any circumstances.

This powerful faculty is with you all the time. It operates whether you think about it or not. Do you realize how imperative it is to have a clear relationship to the mind? I can go on saying many things that you have never heard. The mind is subtle and interwoven throughout our life, our problems, and our excellence.

The mind is tangible, practical, and always with you. You can affect it many ways. It is not something beyond your reach and impact. In a simple layman's statement: "There are two ways to deal with the mind. Either your mind is under you, or you are under your mind." It is blunt, simple, and true.

Whenever you are subject to your mind, you act and become inferior. You begin to say things like, "I can't help my feelings," "I can't understand it," or "I can't believe myself." At that moment you did not use your mind to relate to your soul and vastness. You reacted under the mind and its attachments to your personality, ego, and environments. You are subjected by your mind.

When your mind is subject to you, you act and become superior. You have clarity and deliver your excellence. You think, "I am, I AM," "I trust that I am trustworthy." Normally we think we have something real and of value when we get a few thousand dollars here, or a few million dollars there, or we have a beautiful wife, or ten girlfriends. We believe this temptation or that projection of our mind has some basic value. Forget it my friend! There is no value at all, not even a bit.

Excellence, awareness, and caliber come to you when you make your mind play the game you and your soul want. When you play the game your mind makes you play, it ruins you and creates your pain. The mind is vast and extends throughout the totality of the universe. It is involved everywhere. So you become a victim in many ways. You are a victim of your subconscious, which is part of your mind. You are a victim of your conscience, which is part of your mind. You are even a victim of your absolutely supreme consciousness that also acts through your mind.

When you have an established relationship to your mind, you are aware at all times of the frequency, Projection, Facet, and part of your mind that acts, as well as the chakra through which you act. You realize your mind uses many parts, and that the greater mind has three Functional Minds: Negative Mind, Positive Mind, and Neutral Mind. Your mind thinks, feels, and acts differently in each of these three. They color all your actions and thoughts. Without this awareness and control of your mind, you surrender your own judgments. You let the mind decide for you!

Just imagine your normal condition. You may be speaking to someone about a business topic. Just outside of your central awareness, your mind sends you a stream of thoughts: "You sound good. Actually you sound bad. You lack confidence. You are wrong. You must be right...etc." Who is to judge? Your mind is a stream of thoughts, impressions, and reactions. It is a collection of animal and human faculties under the pressure of the senses and under social pressure. But you are not the mind. That stream of thoughts and reactions is not you. Therefore, your mind cannot judge that you are good or bad, right or wrong, confident or doubtful. If you do not control your projections and action from a point of equilibrium and awareness, then you surrender your judgmental capacity and your identity! Your words and actions lose impact, coherence, and depth.

You have incredible faculties in this human body and brain. But without a relationship to your mind what will happen? You won't have control of your self to face your mind. Then your habits control you. And when your habits control you, you are a robotic disaster. Call that condition anything you like—interlocked neuroses, crippled awareness, stereotyped behaviors. Whatever your terminology, it is essentially a web of habits that rules the psyche and then you.

This happens because the mind has a capacity to act like a recorder. A habit enters the recorder and then begins, automatically, to play itself back in your behavior, feelings, and thoughts. Layer after layer of habit forms in the subconscious mind of each person. Used with awareness habits help you act quickly, and they automate actions that require little change. Used without a relationship between you and the mind, they steal your spontaneity, uniqueness, and projection. You have a choice: live in excellence and awareness or live subject to the stereotypes of your subconscious habits.

If you choose to live in your excellence, then you must take responsibility for your self. You must recognize the capacity of your mind, acknowledge your self, and direct that relationship. We all want to live with excellence and experience love, happiness, and the ecstasy of life. How can we get there? You need a simple mind. You need the capacity for innocence before your own soul. You need the warmth of the heart and the clarity of the head. It is something you cannot buy in the market nor get by holding on to some belief. It only comes to you when your mind has become pure and most simple.

The problem is that without a clear relationship to your mind, the ego takes over. And the ego loves complications. Instead of doing what is necessary and enjoying the fruits of those actions, whatever they may be, you follow the reactions of the mind and create complications. You are afraid and try to control everything. The way you control is by emotional compensations. Instead of creating a clear cause, a righteous action, a potent seed, you want sympathy. To get sympathy you act with apathy, as if you are powerless and are not responsible to act. You want attention, and you try to get it with a shout or a pout! You try anything except letting things progress to success and completion. You have no trust, because you have no clarity and no relationship to your mind. That is the reason a human being, who is created in the image of God, can be surrounded by failure and unhappiness. You act as if nothing is real to you. As if you could act and create without a precise and certain consequence. When you recognize your own basic nature, you recognize the power of your purity, piety, and innocence. You forge a direct and simple relationship to the mind and all its complications.

How can we accomplish this relationship? That is why we meditate. That is why we do *jappa* and *naam simran*. In the world of your mind, you feel, you have emotions, you have habits, you have sensory actions and reactions. You may have control or no control. In meditation you begin to realize that there is a world of you. There is a world of your mind, and a world of you. In the world of you, in your basic elementary situation, in your identity, your mind is your servant not your master. That is why we do Kundalini Yoga. That is why we do *sadhana*.

You are given a body and mind that are designed with the subtlety and power to respond to you and to your soul. Yet you act as if they are insensitive and you have no power. You act without understanding or innocence.

Bhagat Kabir reminded us that:

ਗੁਰ ਸੇਵਾ ਤੇ ਭਗਤਿ ਕਮਾਈ
ਤਬ ਇਹ ਮਾਨਸ ਦੇਹੀ ਪਾਈ
ਇਸ ਦੇਹੀ ਕਉ ਸਿਮਰਹਿ ਦੇਵ
ਸੋ ਦੇਹੀ ਭਜੁ ਹਰਿ ਕੀ ਸੇਵ

Gur sevaa tay bhagat kamaa-ee
Tab eh maanas dayhee paa-ee
Is dehee ka-oh simareh dayv
So dayhee bhaj har kee sayv
　　　　-Kabir, *Siri Guru Granth Sahib*, page 1159
Through the Guru's service the Lord's loving adoration is practiced.
Then alone is the fruit of this human body obtained.
Even the gods long for this body.
So through this body of yours, think of rendering service unto God.

I know it is very difficult for you to believe a man of God. Especially here in America, because so many people who claim to be men of God have cheated you, betrayed you, or misled you. You don't know who or what to believe or not believe. I understand the problem and your anger. In America you are only two hundred years old and you do not have a long, established tradition that can act as a testing stone for teachings and teachers. Without developing your inner sensitivity and without a profound established tradition to learn about your mind and spirit, many things have gone wrong, and things will keep on going wrong. So what can you do? If you feel you can't believe anybody or anything, fine. Don't. Instead believe in yourself. Wake up and go deeply in your self. Master the mind. Get to the essence and process of your own life. Stop playing games. If you find I am wrong in my statements, then try to be right and exalt, elevate, and take care of yourself.

I do not offer this perspective on your mind as a counselor. In the ordinary psychological and psychiatric world you are only responsible to the mind. You must work using rapport to form a therapeutic alliance, and you are confined by time and space since you charge by the minute to do your job. In the spiritual world we are responsible to take the person towards Infinity. We are responsible to the whole self and to the destiny in the person. That is why we are direct. Our guidance may take one minute or many hours. That is why we poke, provoke, confront, and elevate. We must speak in a way that confronts you with your self and that adjusts the relationship to your mind based on your reality, identity, and basic nature.

That is why I tell you to meditate, to do *sadhana*, to conquer your mind, and all its facets and projections. As a human being, by nature, you have the capacity for a very deep understanding and sensitivity. Your mind has the faculty to analyze everything in the shortest possible time, so short it can't even be measured. This faculty is called intuition.

Normally, your mind doesn't work that well. You forget to develop the meditative mind and your awareness. You forget to care for this body as a temple and as a most sophisticated creation and instrument. Your brain cannot compute well because your hormonal and neurochemical base is poor. Then your power, which is in your basic structure and brain, is not facilitated to understand, to analyze in depth, to compute, and reconstruct the thought forms of your entire psyche. Further, you are not trained to use your mind to synchronize your own magnetic field with the cosmic magnetic field, which has a complete interconnection with all other humans, other existences, and realms of material existence. That synchronization gives you guidance and pathways through every problem. Did you know that? Do you know that as an experience, as a practical skill? You, through your meditative mind, should be in the position to control your projection, attitude, and acknowledgement towards the entire globe. Equally you should be sensitive and in control of the entire global acknowledgement projected towards you. You and your mind are that sophisticated and rich in design!

Without meditation, and without a relationship to your mind, you fail to use the power of the mind. You fail to rely on your self. You complicate your approach. You do not use the beautiful designs given to you by birthright in this body, that link the effectiveness of body, mind, soul, and you.

If you are pure and your food is pure, your mind can act well and your entire life can be well. You often do things that stop your built-in cleansing and support functions. You do not know or appreciate how well designed your body and mind are. Take an area of your body you feel is very lowly, and you think does not affect your mind: the area we call the armpit. Normally you worry that that area will create a bad odor. You cover it in layers of chemicals and stop it from sweating. Unfortunately, this diffuses the accurate release of hormones into your bloodstream, which impairs the top functioning of your brain and mind! You block a window that God created and never designed to be blocked. The armpit is one of the most sensitive areas in the body. The balance in the sympathetic and parasympathetic nervous systems depends on the signals from that little area. Is it sweating? Is it moving? What are the chemical signals from circulation, skin, lymph, etc? You read your body from those signals. The normal release from that area helps prevent many medical problems, from impurities in the blood to cancer. If you start to get a bad signal from there, change your diet and exercise. Meditate and calm your reactive mind, reduce your stress. But that solution requires you to act, to have a discipline, to sense your own condition. It means you take responsibility and use your gifts and the temple of the body.

Periodic fasting is well known to clear the mind and to adjust our relationship to many of our emotions and impulses. Take the example of Mahatma Ghandi. He fasted, lived simply, and when he died the entire world acknowledged him. Right or wrong, his mind was coherent and his mind awakened the acknowledgement of the psyche of the entire globe.

When you need energy and want to make the mind alert, you do not need to take drugs. Just take *kaalee cholay* (black grams—a kind of garbanzo bean). It is a delicious food, commonly available, cheap, and beautifully holistic. Prepare these black garbanzos with black pepper, black salt, onions, ginger, garlic, and a little green chilies or jalepeños. Eat them every day. In 40 days they clean your system, and they give you so much energy you feel you can leap over walls. Even nature knows these little beans have a special power. You can identify which fields grow them. Just as the plants reach the middle of their ripeness, when the seedlings turn to flowers and then to a pod, the rain comes and lightning begins to play all over the field. It is a spectacular dance between heaven and earth and it marks that field. There is some secret there between that electricity and this food.

There are many techniques to develop the mind and establish your relationship to it. The psychology of human totality and excellence, Humanology, has classified the approaches to evoke, balance, and use each aspect and projection of your mind and its mechanisms. Food, breath, sound, concentration, and exercise are all tools you can use. I will elaborate many of these techniques and show you how they relate to your mind a little later.

The Age is shifting. We had the Industrial Age, then the Information Revolution, and now we are crossing into the Aquarian Age. This will be the Age of Awareness. We will be overloaded with information and our psyches will become more sensitive. It will be essential for each of us to know our mind and command it with our meditative mind. Without control of those many facets, the undirected mind will create depressions, delusions, identity splits, and a deep core feeling of emptiness. It will be our duty, and a fundamental requirement of our future lives, to meditate and to command the mind.

That is why I just want to talk to you right from my heart. I want to share what I know and have experienced. I want to share with you the beauty, the wonders of the human mind. I want you to understand that your mental faculty is not only a power, it is the greatest power, and it is at your call. I am not sharing this to be a professional lecturer or even to start some industry. I want to share some simple truths, which are timeless, and which let you live wonderfully as a human being under all the challenges we have to face. I know for all my best efforts, many of you will not understand the depth and effectiveness of these truths now. You were trained to prefer emotions and your own fears above simple truth. When you clear your mind and come to the state of fearlessness, then you will understand these truths, their applications, and implications.

I share this with you for the future. When your own lineage and the siblings of your generations understand and study these words, it will serve their consciousness. They will grow and become invincible and unshakeable, and their character will become so pure that they can confront death and life and still smile. Their life will be that of radiance. At that time, the truth spoken today will be understood in depth and worshipped and loved. And don't misunderstand that this is about me. This shall all be true because I only repeat what the Gurus have said. These are timeless truths meant for every person. I simply say it in English and in the grassroots language of every person. I refuse to complicate things for you, because you and your ego are already complicated enough.

If you engage your mind, you can be your real self, and you will realize happiness is your birthright. You will decide to at least try to drop your mind's bad habits to be commotional, fearful, and limited. Try to engage your mind in *sadhana*. Try to get up in the early morning. Try to understand that the time is now and now is the time. Those who feel they love God are fine, but those who get up in the morning for *sadhana*, God loves them. Do you know that God wants to love somebody, too? God created this whole universe just to love. God has a special time available to each of us—when you rise in the 2-1/2 hours before the rise of the sun, the ambrosial hours, and synchronize your mind and heart to praise God, God listens. God feels it so much and falls in love with you so much, that it seems unbelievable. In return that Creator touches you with vastness and cleanses your mind. You become fearless, innocent, and pure. Through that clear mind you can see the light of the soul and from the light of the soul you see the entire universe which is bountiful, beautiful, and nothing but an act of love. We can conquer our failures and win our life if we have a clear effective mind.

May your way always be comfortable.
May the wind of happiness be behind you.
May you understand the strength of your own soul.
May you always be bountiful to help anybody who seeks elevation.
May the hand of Nanak protect you. May the power of Guru Ram Das
always heal you. May the courage of Guru Gobind Singh give you victory.
May the Word of the Siri Guru Granth, give you ecstasy, consciousness, and love.
May this planet Earth be awakened to its dignity
by your higher consciousness and grace.
With this prayer, let every beat of my heart
be with you and bless you forever, ever and ever.
Sat Naam.

2 Win the Game of Life

To win the game of life you must have caliber. To have caliber you must have an Applied Mind. An Applied Mind is a mind that processes everything positive and negative then acts from the Neutral Mind to express you. The Applied Mind uses the Neutral Mind to assess all positive and negative, but does not react on that basis. It acts to cause a cause that leads to the fulfillment of you and your destiny, you and your highest identity.

Your mind is a practical tool. Your ability to use it depends on your depth of experience and understanding of its basic structure and functions. This talk introduces the three Functional Minds and their Projections. The point of this and other explorations is to give you a map and tools to live a fulfilled life of excellence and high caliber. The qualities of mind highlighted are the ones you encounter and must direct every day.

Activity of the Mind

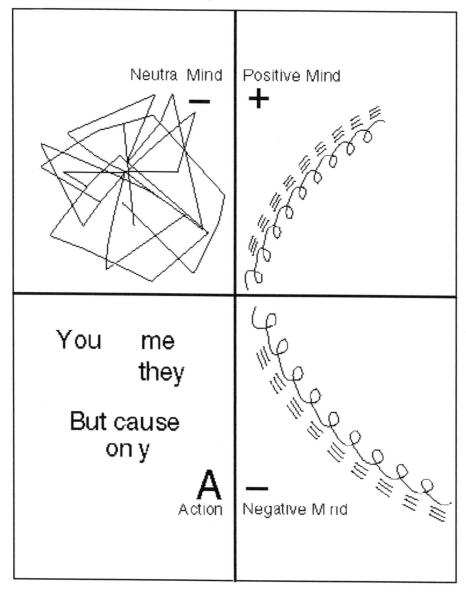

Neutra Mind

Positive Mind

−

+

You   me
    they

But cause
    on y

A

Action

Negative M nd

−

2

THIS TALK THAT I SHARE WITH YOU TODAY WILL BECOME AN elementary course for the human being to excel and be effective throughout all areas of life. These things we will touch on are not some new discovery. These are things that are in you and that are part of your structure. What we are doing is discovering these things within you. When you have that practical experience to relate to your mind and to your self, watch how greatly you can change and optimize your life. You can reach a reality and much higher elevation within your self.

Let's talk this way: you can have any status, title, and degree, but if you cannot deliver what is expected of you and your identity, you are just nobody. Talk will not walk. Saying it is not the same as being it. Hoping and promising is not the same as proving it and passing the test of time. How can you deliver? It can only happen when you have wisdom and you are not empty inside. When you are empty inside, you lack wisdom. When you lack wisdom, you take the help of your ego. Then you become limited, fearful, indirect, and you sell your self cheaply for some feeling or need. Ultimately you become unreal and without true friends.

Let me sketch a diagram for you. *[See opposite page.]* I've drawn two axes so we have four quadrants. The upper right is the Positive Mind (+), the lower right is the Negative Mind (–), and the upper left is the Neutral Mind (=). The final quadrant on the lower left is the realm of your actions (A)—Mind in Action.

Your mind has a very distinct and functional design. Your mind divides into three Functional Minds: Negative, Positive and Neutral. These minds all work at once. They want to know: What is it? Why is what it is? What is happening to me? How is it happening to me? Who's saying it? What is it he is saying? Do I understand? Don't I understand? Do I only think it is so? And on and on. The three Functional Minds process a flood of questions, comparisons, and thoughts.

There are three impersonal areas of the mind. *Manas* is the sensory mind; *ahangkar* gives us identity and attachment; and *buddhi* perceives what is reality. These three interact with the three Functional Minds to give you nine

Aspects, three in each quadrant. Each of the nine Aspects has a triple power on it to experience the thought. The three minds interact with the nine Aspects to give a total of 27 Controlling Projections. So, you have a total of 27 Projections per thought. Your mind churns the thought and turns it many ways. See it on the diagram as I draw the spinning spirals out from the center. One thought and 27 spirals outward. When you master your very basic intelligence, you must know and be sensitive to those 27 Projections. The three minds together with all the Projections give you 81 Facets—81 ways to project into action as a result of how you process each thought.

This "A," which means Action, is on the lower left. Do you know why? Because if you are not flexible and humble in your actions and attitude, it won't matter how wise you are or how great you are. In the end you will punish and beat yourself. In the realm of action every cause has an effect. By the time you act you must have balanced the three minds and become neutral. If you are rude, intolerant, pushy, argumentative, or doubting, no one will abide it.

These minds are very active, very busy. So normally our problem is that we do not hear clearly. We do not see things as they are. We do not even hear our own thoughts clearly! Each thought comes cloaked in a cloud of projections, reactions, and facets. In order to deal with all these Facets, you must be able to speak directly with a Neutral Mind. You need to state clearly your fact.

What do you need to say? Facts! Suppose you say, "This tooth is hurting." This is direct and a fact. Then what would not be stating a fact? "I have a kind of pain in my mouth in one of the teeth." Why is he speaking roundabout? Which tooth? Many questions come with the second statement. In the mind of the person who hears it there will be a question, "Is he truthful?" A person who cannot state a simple fact cannot be trusted.

Experience this for a minute. If you say, "I do not want to listen to you," it's factual. If you say, "I don't understand what you are saying. I cannot listen so well," this is a lie. You cannot use your mind to make a clear decision and communicate it. You cover this up by saying you do not understand. But we all have the capacity to understand. You are not neutral and will not deliver the clear position.

If you say, "I do not like to listen to you," then immediately the question comes back to you, "Why not?" A direct dialogue can happen. The mind can deal direct with the fact instead of with the Projections and twists from it. If you do not deal with the direct reality and instead deal only in the Projections and reactions, then you are not dealing with it as a person. Remember this: You are not dealing as a person, without any ego, but are protecting some person or professional status.

Let's experience this dialogue together. If I said, "I don't want to listen to you," and you asked, "Why not?" Then tell me the answer. Answer the question.

CLASS: Because you're not telling the truth.

YB: No. You may want the truth or a lie. But truth or lie, still no conversation has occurred.

CLASS: I know what you want to say.

YB: No, no. Try to respond in your pure, direct human essence. The question is, "Why not?" Right? Give me an answer that hits the heart and sits there as nothing but a pure gospel truth.

CLASS: *(Many answer, as he shakes his head, "no.")*

YB: Repeat after me, forcefully, "I don't want to hear you."

CLASS: "I don't want to hear you."

YB: "Why not?"

CLASS: "Why not?"

YB: "Because I will have to carry you."

CLASS: "Because I will carry you."

Feel the difference? With this answer the dialogue is complete. When you don't want to hear somebody, you also don't want to argue, to discuss logic, or reason. You would have to take on the other person as a burden and carry him. If you wanted to listen you would be eager, "What? What?" Then the energy would flow between you.

Here is another situation. As I came to teach a class someone came up to me. The husband and wife were fighting. The husband stammered, "Egh, egh, egh." I said, "What are you trying to say? Come out with it."

He said, "I, ah...you know I'm married?"

I said, "I was there when you got married. What is the problem?"

After a deep silence he said, "I...Well, I can't have sex with her."

I said, "Yes, but what is wrong about it? If you can't have sex, don't have it. Is it such a necessity? If you cannot have sex, don't have it."

"But, I am married!"

I asked, "Do you want to have sex?"

He said, "Yes."

I said, "Do you know you have a sixth sense, a sensitivity?"

He said, "Yes."

I said, "Then the first thing to do is relax. Because sex is not in the organ. Sex is in the command center. Here at the brow point. Your pituitary commands your sexual function."

I told him, "You are very tense. When you think of sex your mind is filled with other projections and fragments. If you're going to have sex, you have to relax first. Your mind is turbulent just like the wind; you have to settle it on the reality, the fact of sex."

Still he said, "How can I relax?"

I said, "Meditate. Meditate in a way to activate the frontal lobe of your brain. Then everything will flow. Take that as a rule of the thumb."

Technically, the best approach is to do *jappa*—repeat the words and mantras we use in Kundalini Yoga and from the *Shabd Guru*. To some that looks insane. But we repeat those words for a purpose and a specific effect. When we repeat those sounds, the tongue touches the upper palate's meridian points. This alerts the thalamus and hypothalamus of the brain. We can control the brain's function and level by our use of the *shabd*. We can settle the function and frequency of the mental projections. Then you can relax and be factual and be present. To this day I understand the man and the woman in the story have a good marriage situation.

I'm sharing these examples to show you the power and consequences of your words. Your words affect the mind and your mental facets affect your words. You can control your mind to be clean and clear. Then you can project to some other mind and impact it directly. Without this habit of neutral, penetrating language, you let a person hear you with no real impact, dialogue, or resolution.

Look at the diagram on page 14, which captures the activity of the mind. The thing to remember is that you are not this mind. You are in essence you, and you are neutral. But your mental Projection will extend the thought both positively and negatively. See how the thought spirals outward in 27 ways from the origin, diagonally out into the Positive Mind. It does the same thing down below in the Negative Mind. Notice that the two spirals do not connect. They do not meet! Therefore, when you ask the question, "Am I negative or positive about this?" It doesn't really matter. You by nature are neutral and beyond the mind. Your mind will magnify each tendency and project it using many Facets.

Look how your memory works. Suppose you recall a painful or embarrassing incident. The moment the Negative Mind starts to act on that memory it magnifies the events and tries to protect you. That is its basic function—to give protection to your life. When the Negative Mind goes through all the 27 Facets, then suppose the Positive Mind picks up the thought. It will start to supply every historical incident that supports and expands that pain. A stream of thoughts will come: "You remember that problem back in 1976? And that unfortunate moment in 1995? And what about that incident you read about in the newspaper? Remember what somebody told you last week?" Your Positive

Mind linked inappropriately to the Negative Mind makes you berserk, depressed, hopeless, and undermines your personality effectiveness. It steals away your courage and becomes your worst enemy.

Under all these waves and projections of the mind, your job is: "If I do not reach the Neutral Mind, where I feel and know, 'I am, I AM,' I will not react or move." It is in the Neutral Mind that you can be calm and pure and speak directly in the light of your soul. Then you speak and act from intuition. Otherwise, you fight for territory, defense, and blame. "This is right. This is wrong. I am hurt." On and on. You just talk what you want to talk, what your mental reactions make you say. But you do not speak as you. You are not heard.

To win the game of life you must have caliber. To have caliber you must have an Applied Mind. An Applied Mind is a mind that processes everything positive and negative then acts from the Neutral Mind to express you. The Applied Mind uses the Neutral Mind to assess all positive and negative but does not react on that basis. It acts to cause a cause that leads to the fulfillment of you and your destiny, you and your highest identity.

See in the diagram on page 14 how your projections in the Neutral Mind always come back to the center? They do not just spin off without a center like the Negative and Positive Minds. And look below that in the lower quadrant. This is the Action Square, "A." What have I written there?

"You—me." "I—they." "But cause only."

Action must follow the cause and must satisfy the cause. What is the story of your life in two words? Cause and effect. Cause and effect!

Each cause must have an effect, and every effect honors its cause. Each word is a cause. Every identity is a cause with its own effects and reality. So a teacher is a teacher, not a human. His effect is teaching, not everything else. To identify your identity and act and speak directly from that with a Neutral Mind gives you caliber, success, and happiness. It trains your mind to use its power to serve you.

You will never be hurt. Happiness is your birthright, not pain. The problem is that the reactions of your mind and its facets do not let you belong to anybody or anything. Nor can anybody belong to you. You get caught into commotions and feelings from all the projections of the mind. I want to talk to you. You want to talk to my mind and its feelings and reactions. I do not want to talk to your mind.

You meditate to penetrate the Facets and talk as you, act as you, be as you. You are given this life as a great gift. It is priceless. Enjoy it. Don't judge it, fight it, try to possess it, or control it. Conquer your own mind and live! Act direct, real, and innocent. Create the cause, and let the effects serve you and your soul.

Your mind can be educated. Take your mind and start it on a thought. Have the thought: "Do I have reverence, or don't I have reverence?" Now, I'm telling you how the mind can be educated. Ask if you have reverence or you don't. If you have no reverence, don't communicate. Stop right there. If you do have reverence, then you must revere your thought, and that thought must be honored to prevail and command every aspect of your communication. The creation acts on cause and effect. It will honor each cause you cause unto Infinity, even if your mind does not. So ask your mind if you, not your mind, has reverence. Project a positive reverence, an eternal respect, for everything whether it is negative and unwanted or positive and desired. Show the same reality, compassion, and understanding. If you give reverence to all, the universe will revere you. Ultimately you will revere and trust your self.

When you conquer your mind you can listen to wisdom and let it find deep roots in your mind to serve you, to come to you whenever you need direction. You can also speak that wisdom simply. Such wisdom forms rules for life. If you listen carefully to simple wisdom, it enriches the mind and opens the heart to your own intuition. To complete this talk, let's share some wisdom, some rules to help you live happily and successfully in life. Rules that help you deal with your mind and the challenges of life.

When this little girl was to be married, I was not well, so I gave her ten fundamental points to live by. I said to her, "I am very sick, I do not know whether I can go or I'll stay, but I am going to give you these ten points to live by. If you love me, you shall live by these ten points and you will not be hurt." She's pretty perfect, and if there is something wrong, I question her. But normally she's good, and she lives by these ten points.

These ten points have something to do with our subject tonight. So, do you have your purse with you? *[Gestures towards his assistant.]* She keeps them in her purse. She's happy so far, "touch wood," and nothing has gone wrong with her. She started under the most intense circumstances. I never even listened to her. I said, "I won't listen to you. I am marrying you to this man. Now you go on a honeymoon. This is how a honeymoon has to be done. You come back; this is how you have to live."

Come on, read your ten points. *[See opposite page.]* See, she has made a little card that fits in her purse. Whenever she's in a situation, she takes it out and reads which rule fits. She's the most trained, positive human being. And if she can be that, everybody can be that. Go ahead, read those points, and we will listen and educate the mind.

Ten Principles to Live By
and Avoid Injury to Self

1. *If you don't want enemies, don't have friends.*

2. *Love is not dove.*

3. *Don't be so sweet that people will want to eat you,*
   or so bitter that people will want to throw you away.

4. *Open the lips, sink the ship. That means don't talk*
   unnecessarily.

5. *Excellence, elegance, and grace are the three elements of a*
   human being. If somebody challenges any of these three in
   you, avoid that person.

6. *Only show your strengths, not your weaknesses.*

7. *If somebody says, "I love you," wait for the next step.*
   People use love as a hook. They say they love you, but often
   they're only out to get something from you.

8. *Trust all for nothing. Trust everybody. Expect nothing.*
   Need nothing. Want nothing. Those who trust everybody
   for nothing, Mother Nature and Heavenly Father will come
   through, it doesn't matter what.

9. *Remember your blessings over your weaknesses.*

10. *Don't utter words in friendship that can be used against*
    you in animosity.

She has been with me for over 20 years and keeps notes on what I teach and speak. She summarizes the wisdom most intelligently. Come. Share with everyone. Read some of those notes to us all. *[Again he gestures towards his assistant.]* Your homework from this talk is to listen and to make your mind grasp it. She's reading it; you grasp it. Concentrate. Don't be distracted by your plus and minus and projections and commotions. Let us see. Go ahead.

Here are some highlights or aphorisms taken from Yogi Bhajan's lectures between March and June 1994.

♦ *If you don't love where you come from, you can't love where you are going to go.*

♦ *You have come from the Infinite to merge with the Infinite. Infinity in you is your soul.*

♦ *A plant can't live without roots. Your soul is your root.*

♦ *Love doesn't give you anything but a glow. In the bewitchment that comes of that glow, even a king will bow to you.*

♦ *Never let yourself or anybody down, and never participate in a letdown. Then Almighty God shall never let you down*

♦ *Your biggest enemy is your insecurity about yourself.*

♦ *For some, Earth is a five-star hotel, and for some it is a dungeon. All that matters is how many smiles and hellos you can give to all.*

♦ *Kindness, compassion, and caring with love is real love. That doesn't mean you can't tell someone they're wrong. If they are wrong, and you don't tell them, then you are a coward. That is how you ruin your children. If you don't confront, you can't elevate. Sit down with mutual respect and caring. Then confront. If you don't do this, you are a waste and aren't even acting as a human.*

♦ *More you give, more you'll be like God. More you take, more you'll be a beast of burden.*

♦ *Don't worry and don't hurry.*

♦ *If mind is your control and emotional feelings are your guide, you are not human. You are an animal. Feelings are like waves. A boat doesn't need waves; it needs wind.*

♦ *This is an affirmation for self-realization: "I shall not sell my consciousness. My consciousness is my awareness of my God." The first principle of self-love is that you are not for sale.*

♦ *Where does your love die and you fail and you depart from God? When you are insecure. When you forget, "You and God are One."*

♦ *Every beat of your heart is the rhythm of your soul. The voice of your soul is your breath.*

- *Love is a self-acknowledgment. When you love yourself, you feel so rich, that you can afford to love everybody.*
- *When your human ego is bigger than your spiritual spirit, then you have died.*
- *Even if you have everything and you do not know forgiveness, you have nothing.*
- *Excuses are self-abuses.*
- *Pain and calamity are challenges that give us strength within us and within our prayers. When you are in pain, your prayers become very strong.*
- *The moment you open up to Infinity, you become Infinity. You must enter the Aquarian Age with breadth, quickness, and openness and be noble, courageous, and selfless.*
- *If God wants you to know, God will tell you. Don't question Him; just be.*
- *God within you must have the courage to relate and face the God outside of you. Outside is the reflection. Inside is the reality.*
- *Human love is for one thing only: to love your soul. Then the Infinite world around you will be in love with you.*
- *You are not to be a disciple; you are to be a living discipline.*
- *Never forget God has made you a human. Never misunderstand, He could have made you a snake or a donkey. God made you for a purpose. Those who don't live their purpose, live in pain.*
- *Every tomorrow is today. Leave a legacy and be one with Infinity and then you will be liberated.*

Thank you, that is enough. When you each listen to this, you can measure for yourself how clear your mind is, how much of this whole conversation you grasped, how much you understood, and how much has gone in you and taken root. Each root will sprout to give you guidance and the fruit of life. Knowledge is listened to, but wisdom is taken in. Wisdom takes root in your mind.

Then, when you become neutral, peaceful, calm, and quiet, it sprouts. And what is the fruit of it? Blessings, grace, bounty, and beauty. People will adore you.

You have to learn this from your own mind. Your mind is part of the Universal Mind. Your mind can walk into any mind, read any mind, and give you what you need. Your mind is a very precious thing. God gave you the mind with swings built into it. The mind has the capacity for neutral balance, and it has negative and positive swings. If you stabilize those two sides, then you can weigh everything correctly.

The problem is when people use and attach to the ego, they begin to think they are better than the teacher, better than the officer or authority, better than everybody. So their fantasies become their reality. They lose the foundation to be themselves.

Life is in a balance. The swings in the mind are there to give you experience and to let you discover the you within you. For all those who will praise and recognize you, there may be an equal number who want to slander you. You may wonder, "Why?" That balance and swing lets your standard be tested. You cannot hold to something external. You must find your own depth and test it, confirm it. So, calamity is not a bad thing. Calamity is a right thing. Calamity only tells you that life has a climate, and climate by nature constantly changes. How can you train your mind to handle the calamities?

ਦੁਖੁ ਪਰਹਰਿ ਸੁਖੁ ਘਰਿ ਲੈ ਜਾਇ

Dukh parhar sukh ghar lai jaa-eh

> -Guru Nanak, *Siri Guru Granth Sahib*, page 2 (5th *pauree* of *Japji Sahib*)

You will then obtain joy in your mind and throw away your pain.

Give that calamity to God who has sent it, and take happiness home. Don't think a tragedy is only a tragedy. It is also to test your courage. In this life you have all come here fully equipped. You can face whatever comes in your life. Some people get sick, fine. Some people get healthy, fine. Some people get poor, fine. In every case, you have a chance to experience and deliver your self and to thank God these karmas are paid.

You have this illusion, this *maya*, that nobody will take care of you. No one at all. You forget a basic reality:

> *God gave you life,*
> *Husband and wife.*
> *God will take care*
> *and God will share*
> *Its Godliness with you.*

The swing of life and mind means we meet, we separate, we meet, and we separate. The Guru puts it this way:

ਸੰਜੋਗੁ ਵਿਜੋਗੁ ਦੁਇ ਕਾਰ ਚਲਾਵਹਿ ਲੇਖੇ ਆਵਹਿ ਭਾਗ

Sanjog vijog du-eh kaar chalaaveh, lay-khay aaveh bhaag

> -Guru Nanak, *Siri Guru Granth Sahib*, pages 6 (29th *pauree* of *Japji Sahib*)

Union with Him, and separation from Him, come by His Will.
We come to receive what is written in our destiny.

The world's ways are regulated by union and separation, and the mortal gets his share according to his destiny.

This constant exchange between separation and union are the two basic acts that run the universe. What do we get out of it? We get *bhaag*—joy and good fortune. We get out of it what is us, within us. And if we master the mind, elevate ourselves, and entwine the mind in blessing and gratitude, then we get the bliss and meet the Infinite within us.

ਭਾਗੁ ਹੋਆ ਗੁਰਿ ਸੰਤੁ ਮਿਲਾਇਆ ਪ੍ਰਭੁ ਅਬਿਨਾਸੀ ਘਰ ਮਹਿ ਪਾਇਆ
Bhaag hoaa gur sant miliaaiaa, prabh abinaashee ghar meh paaiaa
-Guru Arjan, *Siri Guru Granth Sahib*, page 97 (from *Shabd Hazare*)
It is my great good fortune that I have met the Saint Guru
in my own home.

Grace, Grace, Grace of that God, and you realize God and me, me and God are one.

This is the beginning of the science of your mind. When you conquer your facets you speak differently, you pierce the veil of projections, you get into a practical relationship of bliss. You become learned. You become a messenger of truth. You become a balanced human being who is loved, respected, and adored.

My Lord God, Creator, bless my grace. Give me the strength to serve.
Give me the humility to surrender, and give me the power to go ahead in life, to
fulfill the needs of those which I can do, imagine to do, or serve to do.
May this life of mine be that of grace, and as a powerful instrument,
to uplift all I touch, see, and I live with. Forgive my enemies and
bless my slanderers and all those who are waiting for my defeat.
Give them the strength that they can test their virtues against Yours.
Keep Your Light guiding and shining on my path so I can walk unto Thy Heart,
with love, with love, with love.
Sat Naam.

3 Choose Your Altitude

Regardless of your history of abuses or kindness, opportunity or challenge, it is within you to direct your mind. You can be a saint, you can be a human, or you can be a demon.

We are entering the Age of Aquarius in 2012, November 11th. It will be a new time. The entire psyche is changing. You must purify the mind, body, and soul to be real, innocent, and sattvic. Elevate yourself to be angelic. This Age you will all serve is an Age of Awareness, an Age of Experience. This transition to that Age began in the Piscean Age. The Piscean motto was: "I want to know. I need to learn." The Aquarian motto is: "I know. I want to experience."

We are at a crucial change of the time—a change of an Age. The basic sensitivity of people to their own psyche and to each other is shifting. Now we must all experience and know our mind so we can choose to act in an elevated and effective way. Nothing less will be acceptable in this Age of Awareness. This is the practical technology to elevate ourselves.

3

NOBODY IN THE WEST HAS SAID IT VERY OPENLY, DIRECTLY, AND EFFECTIVELY: Your *gunas,* your fundamental quality as a human being and psyche, are your own productivity. You choose with each action and thought the altitude of your mind and life. Everything that happens around you and to you is not your *guna,* your basic personality, or your basic quality. Regardless of your history of abuses or kindness, opportunity, or challenge, it is within you to direct your mind. You can be a saint; you can be a human; or you can be a demon. You can act as an animal at the altitude of impulse and ground, as an earthling human at the altitude of feelings and horizon, or as an angel at the altitude of essence, Infinity, and the cosmos. It is your choice.

Each of you has all three *gunas* or qualities in you: an animal, a normal human which I call earthling, and an angel—the sensitive, awakened human. All three are there. When you act as an animal, you ignore your sensitivity. As an animal you act by impulse and necessity. An animal acts in a very focused way. If hungry, he has to eat. If horny, he has to mate. If threatened, he has to run or kill. The impulse is so strong it acts as a unifying force for the psyche of the animal. As a human when you act as animal you are direct, focused, and robotic—ruled by habit and impulse.

When you act as a normal earthling human you depend upon emotion. All you have is feelings, thoughts, and emotions. You can have so many you do not know whether you should act or not, what you feel or not, or even who you are. The more you depend on that flood of feelings as if that is you, you become more and more mentally corrupt. You lose innocence and the clarity of you as you.

When you act as an angel, you are kind, compassionate, helpful, and true to your word. You are peaceful in action and peaceful at rest. You are innocent and direct. You can listen and act in the Will of God and the reality of your soul.

In this way the rule of life is very simple: each day increase the angel in you and decrease the animal in you. That is all that is required. Most people act like an animal or earthling. But you also do the worst thing—you falsify your own quality. You develop a false ego, a false fantasy, and live in imagination about yourself. You are a human, an angelic reality, but you live as if you are an earthworm, burrowing in the earth and darkness! And you are worse than the earthworm. At least the earthworm is what an earthworm is. There is no duality. Your habit is to doubt everything, question everyone. You doubt so much, you fear so much you live in fantasy and cannot learn anything. You do not become wise. A wise person does not question anything. He has a sensory system that is alert and has intuition. He has an understanding that reads between the lines. Duality is when you have a chance to learn and instead you question. You promote your feelings and fantasy but you cannot listen. Though you have a mental quality, *sattva*, to be able to listen, you question intentions, relevancy, ability, everything. That is the worst position of the mind.

Your mind has qualities, and they must support your personality and character. Your behaviors will directly reflect and be supported by the qualities and projection of the mind. There are five earthly *tattvas*—earth, water, fire, air, and ether—that are qualities in our senses and in the world. These engage three kinds of behaviors or three qualities, called *gunas,* that determine the altitude and attitudes of your life. These three gunas are: *tamas, rajas,* and *sattva*.

If your mind is *tamasic,* you will act stupid, angry, dull, and confused. You may have hidden anger or ingrown temperamental anger. That's the worst state of mind.

If your mind has a *rajasic guna,* you will be demanding. You will be royal, positive, and active. For your goals you may make a war, but it's a royal thing with a purpose.

If your mind is ruled by the *sattvic guna,* regardless of conditions, with all things as they are, you'll be angelic, and sail through every situation as a saint. You will be peaceful, tranquil, content, and full of grace, honor, and discipline. Your personality will be perfectly united with your spirit, and you will be nothing but radiance.

Your *gunas* and their qualities of behavior are summarized below:

The Three Gunas

Tamasic—Animal	Rajasic—Earthling Human	Sattvic—Angelic Human
Personality Split	Personality Aligned	Personality Unified to Spirit
Angry, Confused, Stupid	Demanding, Positive, Active	Graceful, Peaceful, Disciplined
Red Spectrum	Yellow Spectrum	Green Spectrum
Impulsive	Emotional, Commotional	Intuitive, Sensitive
God as Existence	God as Companion	God as Personal & Present

Our ancient social history left many habits that do not support this basic *sattvic guna* and sensitivity as a human. Long ago we were just impulsive and separated, like single men. One man had a woman and lived in a tree. We were a kind of barbarian and had to survive. Then we started feeling something new. We didn't like it anymore. We felt empty. So we started living in the caves. In the caves everybody who could come was asked to come. We developed as a cave people. Eventually from the cave, a few caves joined together and we became clans. Then a few clans got together and we became tribes. With more time, some tribes came together, developed socially and communicatively, and became a nation. During the tribal periods we would take over the other tribe. We would conquer it, and put it under our power. We had slaves and we signified status by clothes, habits, and speech. This is when we started to shave all men and women who were used as slaves. We took away the sensitivity of the hair and the dignity of living as God made us. That is why so many spiritual traditions respect the hair and its *sattvic* qualities in the person.

Finally we became nations. Then as nations we used the divine right of kings. Those who were kings were the king. The rest were all peasants with no rights. It was so bad that women were sold in the market for four goats or three sheep. We didn't even have bathrooms. Those instincts and ways of living are still among us. Even with great thought and great civilizations we created gunpowder, cannons, vast war machines, and plutonium bombs. We tribally killed ten to forty million people in each war. And we are still killing and starving millions. In the end we live without sensitivity and create poverty and insecurity. We neglect the need to direct and conquer the mind regardless of what we invent and possess.

That is why you will see the traditions of simple dress and eating lightly. They are habits to support the mind and your basic *guna* as angelic: to walk lightly on the earth; to walk firmly in your spirit. The color associated with the *sattvic guna* is white. To dress with the angelic quality is the practice of *satamber*. It is a very old system. I do not know how far it is true or not true. Only three types of cloth for clothes were suggested: cotton, silk, or wool. Always light or white. The hair was understood and respected. You would not expose your head hair to the sun, because this solar center, at the crown of the head, is naturally covered by the hair for a purpose. These are things which affect you and which they sensed. I'm not telling you something you have to do. I am just explaining some habits of sensitive *sattvic* traditions. They overcame the power of slavery and the inferiority complex of status. They would not expose the head hair directly to the sun unless they were wet, or it was after sunset. And whenever they would go to a synagogue, temple, or sacred place, they used to cover their heads.

We have forgotten our own sensory system and our basic *guna* of the angel-ic self. We react to the environments and act emotionally. We try to manipulate with emotions and feelings instead of projecting an impact from our soul. We do not trust and rely on the angel in us.

All of you can be real, compassionate, and choose to live with altitude. Then you teach. One way or another you elevate everyone by your words, actions, and prayers. If you start to deal only with emotions and feelings and not your heart and self, you will be a tragedy. Have you seen many spiritual teachers in the United States fall? They fell and many were hurt. It's not that they didn't know something nor try to do something good. They fell because they did not understand their role to be angelic and saintly. They tried to be earthlings or they tried to control the earth instead of their own mind.

You must understand this idea of a teacher. A teacher is essential. A teacher is a wake-up call. You Westerners are trained to think a teacher is a bloody slave who lives off your money. You think a teacher informs and entertains. That is why I never initiate anyone. If someone wants to become a student, they must initiate themselves. The student has to rise, become angelic, and become a Teacher. Your idea of a teacher is so wrong. You think a teacher is an intel-lectual baboon. A clone who recites teachings. Learn something fundamental. A teacher is not a person who teaches. A teacher is not someone who knows the teachings. A teacher is that person who by the teachings and his or her impact sets the goals, standards, and *guna* of the person. It is a self-sacrifice. In the West you have never learned the grace and glory of being a true teacher. God has no other way except to channelize through the tongue and heart of some-one called a "teacher." This is true as long as he is not a leecher, but a real teacher. In that person all the *gunas* have to be balanced. The projected Facets of the mind must support the basic *guna* of the person.

That is why real success as a human and as a teacher only comes as you are angelic, as you let go the earth. Feel the earth. Exalt the earth. But do not attach and try to hold to it. It is against a basic law of God and your soul. Have everything, but let it serve your consciousness. That is what a teacher is for. To shake you and wake you.

ਗੁਰ ਬਿਨੁ ਘੋਰੁ ਅੰਧਾਰੁ ਗੁਰੂ ਬਿਨੁ ਸਮਝ ਨ ਆਵੈ
Gur bin ghor andhaar, guroo bin samaj na aavai
    -*Siri Guru Granth Sahib*, page 1399 (*Swaiya* in Praise of Guru Ram Das)
Without the Guru, there is darkness, and without the Guru,
understanding is not obtained.

Without Guru, the teacher, there's an absolute darkness, and no one will have any awareness.

ਜੇ ਸਉ ਚੰਦਾ ਉਗਵਹਿ ਸੂਰਜ ਚੜਹਿ ਹਜਾਰ
ਏਤੇ ਚਾਨਣ ਹੋਦਿਆਂ ਗੁਰ ਬਿਨੁ ਘੋਰ ਅੰਧਾਰ

Jay sa-o chandaa oga-veh sooraj char-eh hazaar
Aytay chaanan hodiaa(n), gur bin ghor andhaar
      -Guru Nanak, *Siri Guru Granth Sahib*, page 463
If a hundred moons arise and a thousand suns appear,
even with such light, there would be pitch darkness without the Guru.

With all that light, still without Guru there is darkness. You can read every book and own every house and gem, but without experience of your soul and fundamental self it is worthless.

That is why if you choose to walk on the path of spirit and people look to you, and then you betray your own spirit and basic *guna*, your fall is enormous. The pain and disgrace is indescribable. You just eclipse, and disappear; become remote to your own soul. The Guru shows the way. Otherwise, it is treacherous and complicated by your own mind and impulses and *gunas*.

When you become *sattvic* there is no compromise. Once a student teacher of mine came to me and asked, "Why won't you compromise with me?"

"Finish your service and don't be emotional."

"We have all decided to leave. And my wife doesn't trust you. And I think we should get money from this land of the ashram. Make some deal with us."

I said, "Listen. I unfortunately must tell you the results of your actions. Your wife will divorce you. All these people you think will follow you will go away. This ashram will not dissolve when you go, but it will become a greater center for service, even international. And lastly, as a teacher I am not a compromise. I will kick you firmly in the backside and usher you out myself. Pack up and go."

Now all those people have gone, divorce occurred, tragedy completed itself. I am fine. I have my strength, dignity, and clarity. They are eclipsed and gone by their own emotional doubt and self-treachery.

To be happy as a human being you must recognize your basic *guna* and live to it. You must have an effective personality. Your *tattvas* and *gunas* must support you. Your mind needs to project in unisonness the power of your facets to deliver your own angelic self. You must call on your own spiritual and genetic strength. You have been given everything you need.

Your word is powerful. It directs your mind. But you make stupid declarations all the time. You make sounds like: "Ooh, ooh, sigh, sigh." You ask people, "What are you doing today?" And instead of declaring themselves to you directly, they moan and make faces, sigh and act like monkeys. They cannot even answer. Or suddenly they throw the arms up in the air— "I'm OK. Let's have some fun somehow!" Just like a snakebite they jump. They grab an impulse and it grabs them. Even animals don't do this. A lion will rise and declare himself. He'll say, "ROOAR!" And tell the whole world, "I am a king, I am here!" It's called "impact." The whole jungle will know he is the king of the beast.

In your basic personality every woman has to know she's the beauty of the universe, and every man has to know he's the star of courage. Instead of speaking that and doing that, you complain, excuse, and avoid: "This messed-up. That didn't happen. They made me miss it. That was done to me. I don't really know what to do." What an insult! That language has no human energy in it! Nothing effective.

Instead of bringing your mind and self to your projection, you seek things out for excitement. You make love for excitement when it already is an excitement, and it is you who needs to warm up.

Look at the animals. Have you watched birds build a home? They make the best homes. Without even hands, just with their beaks they put it together into a beautiful nest. Without all your sophisticated understanding, sensitivity, and subtlety, they can make a better home, and feed the young ones neither too little nor too much. Then they take the young ones and teach them to fly. They teach them the art and power of their genetic strength that came with them. Then they are happy and let them go. Do you teach each other as well as the birds do? Do you teach your children? Do you remind each child and say, "Be the greatest person. Be a universal person. Be vast. Live lightly and forgive all. Listen. Love. Learn. Excel. Live."

Mostly children are treated like furniture. "Sit up. Sit down. Be quiet. Have a toy. Have a grade." But where is the impact in heart, the face-to-face feeling of spirit? Where is the reminder to train the mind and its *guna* to be angelic, vast, and real? Do you just want a money-earning machine? Are you that insecure and emotional? That bound to earth?

There shall be no peace, no tranquility, no real joy in that house. It is against the *gunas*. It is basic. Your fundamental *guna* as a human is that you are angelic and you must rise to act and experience that you are angelic. Eliminate the beast and elevate the earthling to become the angel.

This is a very special chance to be a human and have a human body. You are given the body and the mind to accompany your spirit on this journey.

ਗੁਰ ਸੇਵਾ ਤੇ ਭਗਤਿ ਕਮਾਈ
ਤਬ ਇਹ ਮਾਨਸ ਦੇਹੀ ਪਾਈ
ਇਸ ਦੇਹੀ ਕਉ ਸਿਮਰਹਿ ਦੇਵ
ਸੋ ਦੇਹੀ ਭਜੁ ਹਰਿ ਕੀ ਸੇਵ

Gur sayvaa tay bhagat kamaa-ee. Tab eh maanas dayhee paa-ee
Is dayhee ka-ho simareh dayv. So dayhee bhaj har kee sayv
   -Kabir, *Siri Guru Granth Sahib*, page 1159
Through the Guru's service the Lord's loving adoration is practiced.
Then alone is the fruit of this human body obtained.
Even the gods long for this body.
So through this body of yours, think of rendering service unto God.

With the Guru's grace, in past incarnations you earned this life. You earned this human body. It is prepaid and pre-earned. Everything in this life is given to you as it is. You have earned it with your devotion, with your meditation, and with your good deeds. So be content. Some people are bald, some people have thick hair. Some people are short, some people are seven feet tall. First your destiny was decided, then body was given accordingly. Why do the angels long for this body? Because an angel has to have a human body in order to liberate itself. This body is a qualifying factor. With this body, you have the choice to serve God's universe. You can become a little more angelic, a little less animal each day, each thought.

Every religion and tradition tells you to deal with the feelings. Do not suppress them, ignore them, or stop them. Synchronize, divert, and elevate them. You wonder if we are Jews, Sikhs, Muslims, Christians, or Hindus. Who are we really? We think we are so many things. In reality, practically, we are nothing at all, because we are not ourselves. So, we exploit religions. What good is a religion of that person who is full of anger in himself? He has no religion. He is *tamasic*. His mind is clouded. There is no room for the spirit. A person with a hidden, glowing anger can have no religion. A person with fear and a building insecurity has no religion. A coward has no religion. A person attached and covered in earth has no religion. That is why we are told be without: *kaam, krodh, lobh, moh, ahangkar.*

Kaam means *kaamanaa*, desire. You have to convert it. Desire that you should be an angel. *Krodh*, anger. Be angry that you are not angelic. Correct your habits. *Lobh*, greed. Be greedy to be speedy to become angelic. *Moh*, pride. Have pride and gratitude that God has made you human and that you are going to be saintly. *Ahangkar*, attachment. Practice attachment to those ideals that make you become a saint, a giver, a healer.

Love is a basic capacity in your angelic nature. But let me ask you a question. Tell me honestly, without any prejudice, after you feel and declare love for each other, what makes you to depart? How can you tear that bond when love is infinite? Animals have the right to separate. They are ruled by impulse. So when they are horny they are in love. When they are not, they separate. Now, technically, even in the animal kingdom God has proven that there is a chance to touch and understand each other for life. There is the mystic animal of Native Americans called "wolf." It is one animal that lives in a united union.

You have a short life. What is the length? Sixty-five or seventy-five years? That's nothing. In the cycles of time, the movements of galaxies and in the cycles of lifetimes, it is a flash. And every one of your thirty trillion cells lives, has a life, has a cycle, too. How can you love, merge, marry, and split in a few years?

Your mind is not serving your basic quality or *guna*. You do not have the angelic *guna* vibrating throughout your mental aspects and facets. Without it you only want what? "Oh, we want big houses, a big family, rich environments, a few husbands, a couple of divorces." You have an in-built faculty for sensitivity, but you block it with your egomania. You deny your own nature and cover those intuitions with games of apathy, sympathy, tantrum, and anger.

You do this with your love, with your own soul, and with your teacher. I talked to a student one day. He said to me, "I am avoiding you."

I said, "Well, if you are avoiding me, why are you calling me? Go ahead and avoid me. It's OK."

"I just want to tell you I am avoiding you. Why am I doing this?"

I said, "Don't play the commotional game. You know what you are doing. You are avoiding me. I am not avoiding you."

He asked, "What should I do?"

I said, "Stop acting like an idiot, pretending you are insensitive."

He said, "Is that all you will tell me?"

I said, "I can tell you more. I can tell you that you are an egomaniac and an idiot. You are avoiding me because you know when I will speak directly, I will tell you how corrupt and emotional you are. You don't want to hear it. Instead, you want to gain temporary satisfaction in your anger and ego. But this is going to fly in your face. For God's sake, don't let this chance go, don't avoid your self. It will never come back again. All you know is what emotional satisfaction you are gaining right now. You are not sensing what you are losing for all time. What you will lose will be so painful when you realize what you have lost, that you will never forgive yourself. Now, I have told you, but you still have not heard me. You don't want to listen."

This insane behavior is less than that of an earthling. The mind takes you into the realm you want. Do you understand that with the human body it is a choice? There is nothing wrong. You must have the choice. You can do whatever you want. Make a choice. If you use the mind in the *sattvic guna*, it makes you saintly and enriches you to be crowned as a Lord of the Universe. You are connected and effective. If you use the *rajasic guna*, it empowers you to be the king of the territory. You gain jurisdiction wherever you can feel, see, and live. If you use the *tamasic guna*, it makes a human an animal in this world without any blessings or guidance from the heavens.

Your Positive and Negative Minds spin out with the *tamasic* and *rajasic gunas* and plunge you into competition, comparison, and calculation. You try to manipulate and think your way out of the problem. You seek perfection. You start to criticize your self, your body, the entire creation, and even God! You swing from massive efforts and success to depression and anger. You do not understand the key.

The *sattvic guna* and the angelic quality in you can only be conquered by pure love. There are three acts that can bring you and any saint to that position before the teacher and before God: dedication, devotion and surrender. But these are very hard for an egomaniac to do! There are three people who can accomplish this all the way: One whom God has blessed to do it, one who has consciously blessed himself, and one whom the Teacher has blessed.

When you are touched by Infinity you become that. Everything else falls short. Everything else is earth language only. In my life, I had one example that shocked even me. But I understood this guna. There was a saint, Baba Karak Singh. He built lots of temples and lots of gurdwaras. He was a very skinny guy who used to have a servant, a disciple, named Darshan Singh. He never called him "Darshan Singh." He only called him like this: "Hey Darshu! Darshu-dog do this! Darshu-donkey do that." He would heap five, six abuses in a row—that I can not say—and end with "—Darshu."

One day I met Darshan Singh. I said, "Darshan Singh, I have no right to intervene, but I wonder, can you say nothing when this old man abuses you morning 'til night? All you say is, 'Yes, Sir'?"

He said, "That he calls me at all is more than enough. He can call me any way he likes."

I said, "OK." He was content and understood his situation.

After a while, death was taking Baba Karak Singh. He called out, "Oh, Darshu!" Followed by an abusive name. "Bring me that turban!"

He quickly brought the teacher's turban, without a word.

Baba Karak Singh said, "Help me tie it on your head." He tied it perfectly on Darshu's head. Then he said, "Now you're a saint. Sant Darshan Singh."

Now, he is in fact Sant Darshan Singh. He has so much wealth, he doesn't know what to do with it. His whole life has been purified to the extent that he reacts against nothing and has no desire to touch anything wrong. Now Darshan Singh has to care for all those millions of rupees Baba Karak Singh had sitting there in baskets and never even counted, and he has to tend all those properties and temples.

When I went to India again I met him. I asked, "How do you feel?"

He said, "I miss him."

I said, "But he used to abuse you so much. Does it not feel better to have that off your back?"

He said, "You all look at the abuse. I didn't look at the abuse, and I don't. All I can feel is the constant connection and closeness. I always look at the constant connection."

Then he explained it to me in a story. A very, very Christian story. There was one man on Earth, who used to abuse God directly, out loud, even in his sleep. Every one in the village could hear his abuses in the early morning and late at night. In the tradition of Christianity all the saints and saintly people are lined up, and waiting for the pearly Golden Gates of Heaven to open. The gates opened every hundred years to let the blessed ones in. But on this day, many decades before the hundredth year, they opened the Golden Gates for this old man. The same one that had abused God all those years. He went in directly with no waiting. All saints who were lined up were very surprised and curious.

They asked Saint Peter, "How could that happen? He abused God on earth 24-hours a day, even in his sleep. We worshipped God, praised God, and elevated God at every opportunity. But we have to wait and get processed while he goes straight in. What kind of justice is this?"

Peter said, "Don't worry. On Earth you must have slept sometime, done some important task sometimes, and taken special times off. Is that, right?"

They said, "Yes. We worked, we earned, we did everything."

Peter said, "He always abused."

He said, "That's right."

Saint Peter said, "Well, then that's why he got through the Gate. He was with God 24-hours a day without exception. God doesn't hear the earth language at all. God only hears the language of the heart that told him his devotee constantly paid attention to God—while sleeping, while walking, while living, while eating."

So in love, you have to see God, look like God, and be like God. It is a complete merger. It is the language of Love. It is the sixth sense of this *guna*. That is why a

Christian priest wears a collar. It is his habit. He is a dog of the Lord. It is the same for a Sikh when we wear the *kara* on the wrist. Bhagat Kabir puts it beautifully,

ਗਲੇ ਹਮਾਰੇ ਜੇਵਰੀ ਜਹ ਖਿੰਚੈ ਤਹ ਜਾਉ

Galay hamaaray jayvaree jeh khinchai teh jaa-oh
-Kabir, *Siri Guru Granth Sahib*, page 1368 (*Sloks*)
There is a chain around my neck; wherever you pull me, I go.

Lord, there is a chain around my neck. Wherever you pull me, there I go. That relationship is special. It comes with the *gunas*. It refines and goes on without end. As an angel you dwell in God and God dwells in you. Your altitude is the highest on each step of life. To the animal realm, God is only an existence. To human and earthling realm, God is a companion. To a saint and the angelic realm, God is personal and always present.

We are entering the Age of Aquarius in 2012, November 11. It will be a new time. The entire psyche is changing. Many people will not cross this cusp. You must purify the mind, body, and soul to be real, innocent, and *sattvic*. Elevate to be angelic. Between now and then, those who are still Pisceans can survive a little. But after that time God only knows.

This Age you will all serve is an Age of Awareness, an Age of Experience. This transition to that Age began in the Piscean Age. The Piscean motto was: "I want to know. I need to learn." The Aquarian motto is: "I know. I want to experience." You will have to deliver experience to everyone. And you must deliver the experience to your self each day. That is *sadhana*, and for that we have a technique.

Guide us in this way, Lord. Give me nobility instead of corruption.
Give me reality instead of duality. Give me grace instead of being ashamed without
face. Give me today for every tomorrow that I may not be part of the sorrow.
My Creator Lord, create in me the faculty and the facets of an angelic human
so I can serve all in Thy Name, with Thy Grace.
Sat Naam.

4 Balance the Elements

This connection between the mind and the tattvas leads to several common phenomena. All missionary people, all healers, and people who are zealous to help others get burned out. Counselors and advisors drain themselves, and it is a recognized professional hazard. Why? Because your mind gets involved and locked into the other person. It is called taking on the vibration of the other person.

As we recognize and sort out the Facets of our mind, we can notice how each quality expresses itself in the least of our habits—even in how we eat. This talk links the etheric qualities of our mind to practical habits through an understanding of the tattvas and their functions.

TODAY I WANT TO TALK WITH YOU ABOUT A TOPIC THAT IS NOT IN your education. The relationship between the mind and the *tattvas*. In Western education this does not exist, and in Eastern education it is almost gone. It remains part of our individual experience and part of our mentality.

There is an old story about how the body, mind, and soul came to be. That story tells us how they relate with each other. It begins with the Infinite presence of God. When God decided to come into the Creation to have experience a change occurred. That change came in stages like the gradual changes in the colors of the dawn. In each stage there is a little less Oneness and a little more separateness. That process that makes everything seem separated is called *maya*. Each new stage of separateness has its own qualities. The yogis call each new stage a *tattva*. There are about 31 stages going from complete Oneness down to pure individual atom separateness. The final five tattvas give rise to the qualities of matter and sensations we are used to.

Creation has layers. It is subtle. In the West we pay attention only to the last most dense layer of matter. Guru Nanak and other saints tell us there are worlds upon unseen worlds. The mind senses all those seen and unseen worlds. Each of us must maintain a special balance in the *tattvas* with our mind in order to have a strong body and a unified personality. The quality of our life, our mind, and our health is maintained by the *tattvas*.

The five densest of the *tattvas* are experienced as qualities in the body and in all matter. These essences are called ether, air, fire, water, and earth. The Ether gives you the space to exist and the quality of that space or form. Air gives the movement of spaces, thought, and the life force we call *prana*. Fire powers your digestion and your lifeblood. Water composes most of you and flows with emotions and impressions. Earth gives the final base structure. It is all that is left after the fire of the funeral pyre is done. It is funny. In the realm of *maya* and earth there is a law of polarity that governs our perceptions and desires. The ash that is left from the funeral pyre is the smallest part of you, and yet it is what you spend most of your time and attachment on.

Each soul that comes to this earth has come with a particular combination of *prana* and *tattvas* to have an experience unique to it. Here is how the story of the soul is often told. When the soul was asked to come into a body, the soul refused. God wanted to separate the soul because of His boredom. He wanted to experience Himself. He created *maya* and nature (*Prakirti*) and all that. Guru Nanak explained this very beautifully in *Japji*. You have to read and recite it to really understand its depth. Guru Nanak explains that there was not a separation as just *Prakirti* and *Purkha*—the creation and the soul. That is not how to understand it. *Japji* explains that it is the *Karta Purkh*. Normally it is explained as *Purkha* and *Prakirti*, God and His Creation, as if they are totally separated. In *Japji* it is just the reverse. It is God in the creation and God. So, God is in every atom of the creation and also completely within Himself.

In simple English, when God out of His boredom wanted to create *Prakirti*, to see His own Self, the soul did not want to go. The longing and love of the soul for God was so great. They are the same frequency and being. So it was decided they could not be truly separated. It was agreed that the soul would not accept the *tattvas*, the divisions, and categories that devolved into matter and the creation. Furthermore, the soul could not accept any confinement since it is against its nature. In order for God to have the experience, three things were agreed upon. First there would be a time limit for the experience; that would be regulated by the amount of *prana* given to the soul through the breath. That is why a human being was called a *praanee*—one who carries the *prana*. After a certain amount of *prana* was used, the *tattvas* that gave the condition of the mind and the existence would leave, and the soul would be free to go. That was one condition.

Second, the soul was given a subtle body to accompany it and give it clarity and distinctness. With the *tattvas* balanced, it was agreed that all people of higher consciousness would be completely tuned into all subtle life around them. With this link they could be very peaceful, very unique, and excellent people. Excellent people are those who can look into the fineness of everything. They can understand the implications and connections between things. They can sense the intentions and are less emotional, commotional, and neurotic. So there is a way to experience everything with grace.

The third thing agreed and given to the soul was the mind, given as a vehicle, as a servant. Just like when you marry your daughter and you give her gifts—clothes, money, and a car. In that way the soul was given a kind of vehicle through the power and faculties of the mind. With the mind, the soul can always tune into and experience God. It can always tune back to the Earth, to this moment in time and space. It is also the mind which adjusts the five *tattvas* into a balanced proportion to match your character and activity.

This connection between the mind and the *tattvas* leads to several common phenomena. All missionary people, all healers, and people who are zealous to help others get burned out. Counselors and advisors drain themselves and it is a recognized professional hazard. Why? Because your mind gets involved in the other person. It is called, "taking on the vibration of the other person." You feel them, intermingle, and even adjust your *tattvas* to express those qualities and interact. You can avoid this if you are insensitive and defended by a buffer of ego. But if you are spiritual, it is not possible to be insensitive; the two do not go together. Your mind can get deeply involved in another person. It can also get involved with your own higher consciousness. When that happens and you find the delightful contact with the higher mind, you can become completely at peace and feel that you are all right and nothing can disturb you. That is why men of God often reach a certain stage, and the *tattvas* that support the body and its activities do not mean anything to them. Then they become sluggish. Look at any history of a God man who lived long enough, who was not nailed on a cross too early. In that state you can neglect the body, since you do not feel it or intertwine with it and fail to maintain the *tattva* balance. Your mind plays an important role in this balance and distribution of energy and *tattvas*. It is a role that is unique and manages your destiny as well as your dignity.

When your mind is balanced and refined it serves your soul and consciousness and it mixes your *tattvas* to give you both divinity and dignity. The temperament of your soul is divinity. It is the desire to be good that makes you a human. It is living as good that makes you a sage. You live goodness when your personality is touched by the quality of divinity in you. You always have a choice with all these gifts. You can buy any bait for a price and fall apart, or you can be aware of and act from your own ultimate life.

When you sense your own ultimate life and your mind supports you with all the *tattvas,* you have an automatic consolidated dignity. It is a quality that penetrates every action and word. You must work out the projection and involvement of your mind. It is a powerful vehicle and can take you anywhere. That was the agreement with the soul. Consider in the first cycle of your consciousness in this life, the first seven years. If your mother was very rude, all you want to do when you become a mother is to be more rude to your own children. How can you justify it? Your mother was a mother, that is true. Then you were born. But when you become a mother, you are also an individual, a soul with your own frequency and destiny. You cannot copy your mother and have dignity. You can take the strength of your mother and the strength of your father, but you cannot be your mother and father. Their *tattvas* are *their tattvas*. Your combinations and actions are yours. It is the common mistake of almost everyone. You can learn from and take the strengths of your parents, but you cannot take their actions. In the old scriptures they say this is the dirtiest abuse. It is a form of mental intercourse with your own mother and father. The only thing you must take from your parents is reverence. You cannot take their life. When you take on the style of life of your mother or father and keep it going, it imbalances your *tattvas* and you. You may be intelligent and trying very hard. It happens because you are not aware. It is the balance of those *tattvas* that distributes the *pranas* to live and to act in order to experience your self and your destiny.

The sensitivity and potential of the mind can interlock you and produce this imbalance. That is why we need a special institution called the teacher. A spiritual teacher is not what you have been taught it is. It is not an attempt to sell you on a man or to enslave you. That is your private idea. Sometimes you think a spiritual teacher is someone who is perfect. Sometimes you take him as a father image. Sometimes you take him to be a person without desires. You may even think he is a person who is naked with a loincloth and a begging bowl, who only eats a little rice. That is not true and not accurate at all.

A spiritual teacher is a very well-defined institution with a set capacity and function. A spiritual teacher is one who measures your consciousness and the relationship between you and your consciousness. The teacher is a human being who has reached a mastery to measure the consciousness and the relationship between the self and the consciousness in every individual. Teachers are very refined and sophisticated people. They can sense your *tattvas* and your balance of intention, frequency, and action. A spiritual teacher must be a most wise, sensitive, compassionate, and absolutely authentic human being who can give you the measured assessment and correction. When you are not aware and do not project from your consciousness, then you are away from your godliness, and you are off of your dignity.

Your mind and your *tattvas* are linked and give certain virtues to your body. Each area of your body is controlled by different *tattvas*. Your mind will feel different, act different, and record differently in each area. If you touch your knee, your navel, your chest, and your forehead, each will react differently. The most sensitive area of ether in your body is the hair on your head. Those fibers should be cared for. They should be combed and oiled so they are soft, silky, and act as antennae for that area. It is your subtlety and clarity in your mind.

You can watch any habit and see how the *tattvas* interact and how people hold their mind and relationship to their consciousness. There is a wonderful habit called eating, and there is a *tattva* imbalance we call "the eating habit disease." People who do not have dignity and self-respect cannot sit down, do a prayer, and be respectable when they eat a meal. You can measure a person's sense of self-respect by looking at this one habit—how they eat.

In an ashram where I taught yoga I asked every one to come and join us at our meal. Each person was to serve himself. At that time I saw a beggar come. He had come to the class to catch certain lessons. So he joined us at lunch. He came, he cleaned the place where he would sit. He put some water all around to purify it. Then he made a place to sit very properly. Then he served the food in an aesthetic, even decorative way. Only then did he sit down to eat. When he sat down, first he did a long prayer. Then he began to eat. I went to him and asked, "What is your profession?" He said, "Unfortunately, I do nothing but beg." But I saw him three days later and he had washed and looked very good. I had a faithful assistant who I asked to go and pick him up. So he picked him up and inquired all about him. We found out that he was deeply lovesick. He was a millionaire who owned six factories. He was well read and had a Ph.D. from Harvard University. His mind had changed its focus from everything to nothing. Even in that state his basic *tattva* to respect himself came through in how he ate.

That is the most important posture of meditation. How you position your self when you eat. It should be meditative eating. People who cannot stand having a good day, who stop before reaping the benefits of a success, cannot eat properly. It is very animalistic to just live and react. Be alive as a human. Dress meditatively. Move meditatively. When you tie a turban, do it well because it takes a king to crown himself.

The mind can submerge itself in sensations, attachments, and possessions. You become forgetful and lose your balance. You focus on the known and the external. You grab and grab, then get buried under all you have grabbed. It makes you unconscious like in a fitful sleep. Once the sun told the moon, "I love you. Come near to me." The sun fell in love and as it came near, the Earth came in between and eclipsed the sun. If even the mighty sun can forget to be conscious and get eclipsed, what will happen with you?

You need a practice to be conscious and to adjust your *tattvas* to act with dignity and divinity. It is my prayer and understanding that some of you are ready to look into the unknown areas of your greater self. You want to experience that refined and subtle nature of your ultimate self. I want to share a meditation that will regulate your mind and *tattvas*, that will keep your mind clear and friendly. *[See Meditation to Command Your Five Tattvas on page 152 in the Meditation Guide.]* Instead of being afraid of the Unknown, make the Unknown your friend. *Sat Naam.*

5 Eliminate Mental Intrigues

The combined strength of your thoughts and your subconscious catches you. This combination, when the subconscious links with the play of the mind, is the origin of mental intrigues and most of your self-defeating patterns. You need a habit to relate to your mind. Sit with your mind and review it, polish it, and direct it.

Your mind has many parts. There is a specific way those parts work together to process thoughts. When the parts are not synchronized properly, your thoughts become entangled in the powerful, automatic functions of your mind. You are caught into the intrigues the entanglements themselves create. One thought can be so intense it seems more real than your own self. This talk sketches the mechanism of intrigue and how to free yourself from it.

5

YOUR MIND MUST NOT INTRIGUE YOU AND ENTRANCE YOU INTO ITS intrigues. The mind must serve you. The mind has to be developed to give you supportive strength. There is no reason to be unhappy other than the pain you get from the results of these intrigues. I have never been unhappy, neither in America nor in India. I don't believe anyone here wants to live unhappily or do anything wrong or corrupt.

You know better than to be unreal and to play games. You know if you lie and play games that it will come back to you ten times stronger. Then why do you act wrong? Why do you engage in endless petty games? You do it because your mind is ruled by mental fogginess. That fogginess comes from the power and craftiness of your mental intrigues. You have intelligence and common sense, but you don't meditate regularly to clear out the mind.

When you fail to meditate, the combined strength of your subconscious and your thoughts catches you. This combination, when the subconscious links with the play of the mind, is the origin of mental intrigues and most of your self-defeating patterns. You need a habit to relate to your mind. You need to sit with your mind and review it, polish it, and direct it.

You do not need to invite in an enemy or call on bad luck to have trouble in your life. You are already in trouble when you let your mental intrigues go unchecked. If your inherent creativity expands that intrigue, your mind will spin it, magnify it, and spread it in every direction. It will weave that intrigue into your words and then project those words to every part of your mind. The result is you lose track of your real self and become shallow, hollow, and full of games. You lose your power of prayer. You lose your innocence. There is no one who can save you from this mess other than yourself.

Your ability to get into trouble was given to you at the same time as your ability to excel and be great. It started in the very beginning. When your soul was sent to this beautiful planet it was to test your love for God and for your truth. God said to your soul, "I gave you the gift of the mind."

Your soul said, "Just one mind with one power?"

God said, "No, as many minds as you need to do any action. Each part of the mind will have its own positive power as well as its own mechanism and intrigue."

The soul asked, "What can it do for me?"

God said, "When you are on this planet Earth, you will be subjected to time and space and constant tests. But your mind always has the capacity to act beyond time and space. Simply direct it toward me."

The mind is a vast, automatic mechanism that processes thoughts and sensations. When you focus on a thought and gather its associated thoughts —a double thought—the mind produces feelings. When your creativity spins out even more thoughts about the feelings and thoughts, the mind produces fantasy and imagination—a triple thought. All these thoughts, feelings, and fantasies mix, contrast, react, and project. The mind flips and twists. It changes perspectives and intensifies each sensation. Without any effort on your part, the mind produces many intrigues.

Your mind is constantly in motion. It produces every kind of thought. It has no base or fundamental reality on its own. It requires your direction. In order to act and create you must use the mind, but the mind can also use you. It can convince you of something, encourage you, then abandon you when it is wrong. Suppose you start to act on a bad thought. The mind encourages you. It tells you your idea is the best opportunity. Your Positive Mind stacks up many examples of similar ideas and the good that could happen. It does not give you a critical comparison to the problems that could happen, and it doesn't ask how this idea is related to you and your purpose. When a tragedy finally happens the mind suddenly tells you, "You were the one who did something wrong. You did a bad job. You are not worthy." The mind that brought up the plan and supported you now judges and condemns you. This creates a guilt concept. That guilt weakens you emotionally. You begin to feel small and out of control. You followed it, got caught in its impulses, and tangled in its intrigue.

Unnecessary guilt is only one of many of the mind's intrigues. More frequent and debilitating is the feeling that you are limited and inferior. The reality is there is nobody who can limit you. There is nobody who can damage you. Your existence is not bound in time and space. You always have a choice of how you project your mind. How you project and how you communicate to your self and to others is your fundamental strength. You can project your mind to a concept and capacity with unlimited scope, vastness, and cosmic unlimitedness. If you act limited because of the environment or because of an emotional reaction, that is a weakness. If you act intentionally to limit your own self because of your knowledge of some consequence you want to avoid, then that is a strength. The mental intrigues that come from your attachments and fears limit your projection and block your vision of what is possible. As soon as you oppress your mind as if it is fixed under time and space, you will feel depressed and cut your self off from your intelligence.

Sometimes you sense when you are caught by your mental intrigues and feel limited and small. You react and try to expand any way you can. You may try to blow apart the feeling of limitation by stimulating the mind with drugs or with some type of extreme or extraordinary experience. That approach just causes more problems and pain. Anything that pushes you up and out instantly and unnaturally will have a powerful reaction of at least equal force that pulls you down and back in. Your efforts will backfire. You can't become spiritual or wise overnight by some grand effort. You cannot be impatient and greedy and gobble God like It is a cookie.

To stop the games and mental intrigues and to truly be happy you must develop a consistent attitude of human life in which you can excel above time and space, using your mind at the frequency of your soul. That is the attitude of a happy person. Every other approach and short-cut will prove to be false. Any approach that relies on holding onto some aspect of finite time and space will fail because time and space constantly change. Everything that changes will always create duality and paradoxes because of the Law of Polarity and Complementarity. That is why you have a deep and profound instinct to feel the Infinite in you, a spiritual longing. The One that you all worship and love and that you want to be is also that which never changes, is beyond time and space, and is always present.

The first signal that lets you know you are in trouble with your mental intrigues is the feeling that you have to confront your own mind. It happens when you begin to feel you cannot handle a situation, and suddenly you are here and your mind is over there. Nobody wants to lose his or her grip on a situation. It is threatening and you react immediately. You and your mind confront each other. The mind is the only tool you have. Whether you succeed or fail, you do it with your mind.

Recognize that your mind has its own nature, virtues, and mechanisms. It has both a Positive and a Negative Mind. Let it have the swings and polarities that come with the play of its parts, but do not allow it to confront you. When you confront that which gives you your strength, it only creates confusion, weakness, and mistakes.

Instead of confronting it, what should you do? Train it. You can train a dog. You can train parrots to walk a tight-wire and fire a toy gun. Monkeys are trained to help the disabled; they serve, also as the best human assistants. What about training your mind? The best approach is to apply the mind. When you apply the mind it becomes engaged in the task or the experience you give it, so it won't confront you. Talk to your mind. Create a relationship to apply and engage it. Tell your mind, "I am the source of God. I am the soul within myself. I am living with the light of God, therefore, you must go with me." Create a partnership with your mind.

When you talk to your mind assess it. Don't be anxious or afraid. As you start talking to it, it will stop working on its other games. This mind is the biggest game player in the world and it's right within you. Once you have a relationship to it, it listens and it cannot play a game to slip something past you or to skip over you. It cannot do anything to you. You begin to use it and ultimately to master it. When you master it you will become masterminded. That marks the beginning of the era of happiness.

The real game is for you to make your mind follow you, so you can become a sage. If you choose instead to follow your mind, it will make you crazy and weak. In this game mastery is the goal and your main enemy is stress. When you are under stress you begin to lose your mind slowly, to a very polite degree. Your mind starts to wander on its own. It looks elsewhere for shelter and hope. It looks into your subconscious and pulls out of it every memory and every fragment of intentions and actions left incomplete in your life. You begin to live in the past. You do not act in the present but according to overlays from your past. When you cannot sense the present and you cannot connect to the future, life becomes very difficult. It is exactly that day that you are confused, and you lose mastery over your mind. You suddenly feel that you cannot meditate, do *sadhana*, or anything else to clear your mind. You start to feel bad and you want to defeat yourself, so you pick up every habit that makes you not prepare your self for confidence and success.

Do you understand how this stress pattern works to lock you into the mind's intrigues? It turns the three minds against you. The mind has three powerful functions, the Negative, Positive, and Neutral Minds. Because you have earned the right to this life, you have the Negative Mind to instinctively protect you. It alerts you to something that is wrong or is a threat. The way the mind intrigues you is to combine its thoughts with your subconscious and with your attachments. When the Negative Mind gives you a thought, normally the Positive Mind should tell you what can be useful or right about that same thought. It should provide a contrast and comparison. Instead, when your mind is full of intrigues, it begins to pull every memory from the subconscious that supports that thought from the Negative Mind. This produces a stream of thoughts, one stacked on top of the other. "It was dangerous then. Yes. It was also dangerous in 1961, 1963, 1972, 1978, 1982, etc." Each repetition of similar feelings increases the intensity of the thought and convinces you that it is real. Your Positive Mind has access to your subconscious and can use it to expand a thought instead of contrast it. If it acts this way you can never reach your Neutral Mind to know who you are and what to do. The Positive Mind should say, "Well, this is the positive side of the real and apparent dangers." Then your Neutral Mind can say to you, "That is the negative and that is the positive, but this is you in relationship to all of that."

You must develop the mind, through meditation, to give you the positive of the negative and the negative of the positive so that by your own grace and consciousness you can find the neutral of it. In this way you can reach to the subtle, refined, and spiritual dimensions of your life and your relationships.

Why not play one game to become timeless and one with God? That is the game of how you recognize and love your own deep truth in life. When you can play just one game that is boundless in time and space, then all others stop. The measure of the game is how near you are to your own truth, to the reality in your soul. How much consciousness and control of that truth do you have? You will be happy in your life in proportion to the degree that you have a handle on that truth, and that you are willing to pay for that truth, and that you commit to and love that truth.

If you go along with your mental intrigues, you will not get spiritual and have worldly success or happiness. You cannot reach that happiness and contentment no matter how many sophisticated intrigues your mind creates. Only two things will work: your presence and your unlimited projection.

You have not learned how to depend on the unseen and unlimited within you. Your soul has a fundamental property that when aligned with your mind gives you impact, intelligence, and effectiveness. Its fundamental property is to be *saibhang*—a self-illumined, aware, and radiant identity of God. It is not subject to anything. This has been a known fact, explored and experienced for centuries. The soul is a slave to none. In fact, everything else is subject to the soul and connected through its projection. So if you call on that and dwell in that, it works where no logic, reason, or mental intrigue can.

Once a counter clerk refused to charge a customer any money. The manager noticed this and asked, "Why didn't you charge that money?" The clerk said, "Don't worry, I am not crazy. Her presence was more satisfying than any amount of money. I decided to give the thing she bought to her as a gift. I will not charge her, and I will pay the money." Then he rang it into the register. This is how presence works in a very ordinary circumstance. Your presence automatically calls on resources through the greater field of the mind.

You might have met people while travelling. You look at them and just say, "Wow!" You don't know anything about them. Inside them there may be emotional time bombs, but their presence alone immediately impacts you. They seem to have a kind of halo around them. Actually, every person has such a light around them which we call the aura. The light of the aura is directly connected to the power of your soul through a subtle structure in the aura. That structure appears across the upper forehead from ear to ear. We call it the arcline. It does for you by radiance what you cannot do for your self by any effort or manipulation. It is penetrating and definite. That special advantage that comes from the power of that light is built by staying with God. It comes from looking through the window of your mind to your soul. When you stretch the Projection of your mind to reach the Infinite, to dwell in God and to abandon its cleverness for innocence, then everyone and everything senses that presence and wants to serve it. The *Siri Guru Granth Sahib* refers to this type of experience:

ਏ ਮਨ ਮੇਰਿਆ ਤੂ ਸਦਾ ਰਹੁ ਹਰਿ ਨਾਲੇ
ਹਰਿ ਨਾਲਿ ਰਹੁ ਤੂ ਮੰਨ ਮੇਰੇ ਦੂਖ ਸਭਿ ਵਿਸਾਰਣਾ
ਅੰਗੀਕਾਰੁ ਓਹੁ ਕਰੇ ਤੇਰਾ ਕਾਰਜ ਸਭਿ ਸਵਾਰਣਾ
ਸਭਨਾ ਗਲਾ ਸਮਰਥੁ ਸੁਆਮੀ ਸੋ ਕਿਉ ਮਨਹੁ ਵਿਸਾਰੇ
ਕਹੈ ਨਾਨਕੁ ਮੰਨ ਮੇਰੇ ਸਦਾ ਰਹੁ ਹਰਿ ਨਾਲੇ

Eh man mayriaa too(n) sadaa raho har naalay
Haar naal raho too(n) man mayray dookh sabh visaarnaa
Angeekaar oh karay tayraa kaaraj sabh savaarnaa
Sabhnaa galaa samarath suaamee so kio manaho visaaray
Kahai naanak man mayray sadaa raho har naalay
   - Guru Amar Das, *Siri Guru Granth Sahib*, page 917 (2nd *pauree* of *Anand Sahib*)
Ever abide with your God, Oh my mind.
He shall make you forget all sufferings.
He shall own you and shall arrange all your affairs.
The Lord is Omnipotent to do all things. Why forget Him from your mind? Says Nanak, Oh my mind, ever abide with your God.

This is the key to training the mind. Use the mind to project to and stay at a point beyond the mind's own nature. When your mind stays with the self-illumined soul within you, then all pains and suffering disappear and your presence radiates and works. If you try to train your mind by confronting your ego and desires, it only causes pain. Train the mind by directing it to confront your unlimited soul. The mind will be elevated, and you will be elevated. That consistent projection and training is called a permanent state of bliss.

Your mind is your projection. Your mind is not your confrontation. When you get mad, that is the time to remember this. Every problem in life, spiritual and non-spiritual, starts when you confront your own mind. If your mind is with you it acts as your leverage, it is your powerful friend. Then you can confront the whole world. *Man jeetai jag jeet—one who conquers his mind has victory over the entire world.* You all want to win the entire world. The world is meant to be won by you. The cosmos is set up so that it is possible for an individual's magnetic field and mental projection to imprint and prevail on the universal magnetic field. When you know this as an experience, integrity and innocence replace your intrigues.

Many great people have found this secret of the mind. They put aside the intrigues. They penetrated the cosmos with a simple, singular projection and never varied regardless of what circumstances, time, and space brought to them. Our culture records their accomplishments. You may forget many things, and you may not be a Christian, but when things go wrong you call on the energy and spirit of Jesus the Christ. You may call with reverence or more profanely with your pain, but you call! You call on that name because it is part of our culture now. He penetrated with love for all. He saw God in every heart. He had no degrees. He was an assistant carpenter. Now so many buildings are built for him. You might forget great royalty like Queen Victoria, but you will always remember Shakespeare. He produced many things, and he penetrated into the very heart of each person and into the common language and emotion of each person. It only takes a few bacteria to make a huge amount of yogurt in a culture. It only takes one clear mind that acts beyond its intrigues to seed the world with truth.

Sat Naam.

6 Look Through the Mind's Window

You should always remain you. You are supposed to remain you, come what may. That is the actual strength of your mind when it is clean and clear. But you do not handle the mind right. You distort the ego first thing. Instead of handling the ego, its attachments and duties simply as they are, you overstretch the ego. You inflate it and deflate it until the window of the mind is like those funhouse mirrors. You overstretch your ego, you attack it as it is, and then you cannot handle the inflation and stretch.

Now you are caught in the game of mind and ego. Between the two, you can be stretched until nothing is left. If you can remember this one little thing and take it to heart, then you can solve your problems one hundred percent. Just remember: the mind is given to you, you are not given to the mind.

This talk shows you how we open or close the window of the mind. It demonstrates the process of ego inflation and deflation that we constantly use. It asks us to evaluate our factual condition and roles and to deliver our self with caliber and consciousness. It shows in plain language why we can sense what to do and yet still go off the track, even in the spiritual world.

6

IN THIS SERIES OF TALKS, I WANT TO SHARE WITH YOU A FEW CONCEPTS and some practical techniques that open the window of your mind. These are things that you as Americans don't know at all and that people from India once knew and have forgotten about. These are fundamentals to live a happy and meaningful life. With your mind you can view every thought, every feeling, and every part of your life. But you can cover that window with so much dust from your ego that you cannot see your soul at all. You can forget your own concept, standards, and who you are in the reality of life.

Each of you knows that when the body is not cleaned, it eventually stinks. To prevent that you shower and clean yourself every morning. It is an act of self-respect and a duty to your consciousness. Do you know it is exactly the same with the mind? When the mind is not cleaned, it eventually stinks. So much dust can accumulate you cannot see anything at all and someone will smell the stink if they just think of you! The entire house of your personality gradually becomes a garbage dump if it is not cleaned.

You, the real you, can never ever be impure. You can never be broken, incomplete, or a sinner. All these feelings and phenomena are the result of your mental facets and projections. They gather together and form a mental break-out, an identical identity that is not real. The fact is, you are a part of the soul and the soul is a part of God, and you are alive because there is a soul in you and you have the energy of *prana* to live. That is it. But you don't agree with that. Why? Because you get caught in your emotions, your traumas, your emptiness, your success, your ambitions, your imagination, and God knows what else.

What is it like to have the mind clear so you can see through it without distortion? It is very easy to feel and say, "I am very happy." It is also very easy to feel and say, "I am very unhappy." In reality you are neither happy nor unhappy. "Happiness" and "sadness" are your mental concepts. They are constructions of your mind and its projections. When the mind is clear it serves you. If you are unhappy, your mind should give you the way to be happy. If you are happy, the mind should just remind you that there is a possibility to become unhappy. It knows that every day is followed by a night and every night is followed by a day. This constant play of the polarities in life will never cease. Your mind should give you balance and applied intelligence to act. It is a mental problem when you try to fix on one extreme of emotion and hold the entire universe still. You can never always be happy and you can never always be unhappy. You must see and understand the fluctuating pros and cons, and then live through the diagonal on the line of the soul and reality between them. A clear mind helps you walk that diagonal path and be consciously you.

You should always remain you. You are supposed to remain you, come what may. That is the actual strength of your mind when it is clean and clear. But you do not handle the mind right. You distort the ego first thing. Instead of handling the ego, its attachments, and duties simply as they are, you overstretch the ego. You inflate it and deflate it until the window of the mind is like those fun house mirrors. You overstretch your ego; you attack it as it is; and then you cannot handle the inflation and stretch. Every unhappy person has overstretched the ego. Normally, somebody comes and butters you up. They bathe you in compliments and kisses. They pump you up as if they had a foot pump [air pump], and you let it happen! You agree because it momentarily feels good. And if somebody comes and deflates you, drags you down, and drenches you in abuse, rumor, and doubt you still agree. You forget your own reality and dignity and become entranced by those projections out of fear, out of subconscious anxiety, out of many things. They tell you that you are miserable, and you are. All that overstretching and understretching is someone's version of you. It is a mental concept and projection. Your subconscious and ego accept it. You become that other version of you. If God would have created you to be somebody else's version of you, then you would merge into somebody for two hours and come out different. That is not what you are, nor how you are constructed to be. That is your mental distortion.

Look how this works. Did you know that whenever a president of the United States retires, he risks going berserk? He was in a job for a few years and starts to feel he is the lord of the entire universe. So when he retires, they make him feel that he is still a president. They always call him "Mr. President," they keep him informed, and they even give him a temporary office and security guards. He is no longer president. He is not even a constable. He served and now he is out. But no one can respond to this fact. It can't be done. A copy of every key report that goes to the real president goes to this guy. Every one knows and has a use for the fact that his ego became so big, that his chair is next to God's. You are kept alive in your old position in your imagination for years and years. But he cannot go back. The four-year job is over. That is exactly the game of the ego: to keep you in place doing things you no longer do. Once you are stretched, you don't want to go back to your accurate size.

This tendency to distort and inflate is a mental dependency that takes you beyond any reality, and that happens in every arena. It takes you beyond your fact, beyond your factual life, and beyond your consciousness to be you. You may think the spiritual world is somehow immune to this. That is not true. It is the worst of all. There are many ego trips in the spiritual world. And spiritual ego is one of the worst, most intractable of all egos. One trip is to always separate your cash from your pocket, as if the dollar was a currency in the heavens. Another is indirect buttering. Very few spiritual people speak to you straight and blunt. I am not very young now, and I have seen very, very few. Most speak like this, "Hummm. Yeah, I see you are a beautiful and wonderful person. I feel a great light around you. You must be a healer and had great past lives." They inflate your spiritual ego and make it even harder to see through the window of your mind. It doesn't help you with the job of cleaning. It is better to tell the student what they need to do. Just tell them, "You are an idiot. You are doing a terrible job. You act nonsensically. Don't do this with your life. But if you choose, go ahead and walk your own way to hell. But if you want to change directions, this is the way to be clear and go towards the heavens. Thank you very much." If they leave ten dollars, fine. If not, that is fine. You did your job and that is it. You engaged them, looked at them clearly without distortion, classified the problem, computerized the answer and direction, and shared it. The matter ends. *Sat Naam, Wahe Guru.* Gratitude to God and Guru, there is nothing more. Job is done.

I have heard people in every church project their own inflations and distortions on every teacher. Someone listed everything he believed Jesus did. I listened and finally had to say, "What did Jesus the Christ really do? You talk like an idiot. Why don't you do what he did? He didn't talk this way about himself. Jesus Christ did a lot of things and didn't do a lot of other things. But one thing he did for sure. He won everybody through the heart, through compassion, and love." Beyond that actuality he doesn't exist. You can stretch it and make a big deal, a huge construction around it. He lived a simple line of life with an impact and legacy. I hear the same about Guru Nanak. Guru Nanak said this, said that, had this miracle and that. Guru Nanak said one basic thing: "Live in truth." Beyond that Guru Nanak didn't say a word. He lived it and his words lived it.

Somebody brought me over eighty volumes of Buddha's work. It was a carload of books. I said, "Thank you for the gift. Am I supposed to read all that?"

He said, "Yes."

I said, "I can already tell you what is written in them."

He said, "Please, tell me."

I said, "Buddha said one line. 'Let your *buddhi* guide you to the *sattva.'* Let your wisdom guide you to truth."

He said, "That is true."

Buddhi means wisdom. *Sattva* is the purity and truth. That is all Buddha said, not a word more. While he lived people tried to inflate his statements, but he was wise.

They asked him, "Do you believe in God?"

He said, "Did I say so?"

Then they asked, "Well, is there no God?"

He said, "I never denied it either. Leave me alone." His conception was very simple and true.

Mohammed actually said only one thing, "Be humble, humble, humble before God." And yet so many things are said about him in the service of every spiritual ego.

The spiritual world is not calm, quiet, and peaceful. It is not a special realm that is minus ego and minus the mind. Everybody who wears white robes and has a long beard like me is just saintly and godly. That is not true. They are still people, and they must still deal with the mind and the ego. You can have ego. That is not the problem. It comes with living. It comes with the vibrancy and polarities in life. The problem is when you go with the ego, inflate it, deflate it, and depend on it. I don't want to offend your ears with something I should not say. You all know what happens to any meal, even to a gourmet meal. It goes through you and ends up coming out in the rest room. No matter how inflated the gourmet and grand the meal, it will come through the same as a humble meal. Then you press the button and it goes down the tubes with water and runs through all the pipes to be processed or to end in the ocean. If you have to go with it, through all the pipes and darkness and smell, it is a long and dangerous journey. You should just let it go! It doesn't matter what the meal is and it doesn't matter what the words are, spiritual or political or economic. It is not you. And you must find a simple diagonal line of life through it.

Your spirituality is basic and authentic. Its natural authenticity does many good things for you. What supports and carries you through challenge, temptation, and pain? It is not my money, not my friends, not my power, and not my status. It is the light of my soul that can carry me. It is my statement, my depth, and my impact from the heart. You think it is your environments and the things in those environments. You put a huge amount of energy and time to create those environments. But then you become a prisoner of them and they will never carry you anywhere. The security you thought they would provide turns out to be a blind spot. It is called mental duality. With no duality, with innocence and genuine spiritual integrity, you flow with the flow of your spirit. Then your mind will just serve you and life will be creative, elevated, beautiful, and authentic. And when it is authentic, you will be trusted. You will be direct, speak the truth, and never need to manufacture anything negative to manipulate or control anything.

Mostly you train your mind to listen to "inflations." You love the pleasing sounds that praise your ego. That is why Guru Amar Das, the third teacher of the Sikh path, said, "Oh my ears you were meant to hear the Truth." These ears listen so much to inflated lies they can not recognize the truth when it is spoken. If the window of the mind is dirty, if the mind is shallow and you have not refined it, then you can speak truth to such a mind and it can not hear it or take it in to experience.

Life has become a "I-love-you, I-don't-love-you" game. You do not actually love, nor do you hate. There is no truth in either one. Love itself is blind. It is beyond pluses and minuses. When you are in love, how can you see if somebody is nice and beautiful or not? You can't see a thing. When you are in love, you just love. You don't think, "Oh, I love your tan body." How can you love because of a tan body when you can't see at all? Love is a faculty of the spirit, and it does not know a limit or a definition. A young girl told me her story. A man told her, "You are very beautiful. You are pretty. Your body is perfect. You are my darling."

She loved all that, and so they made love together. Lovemaking was very good, they were fine, they had a good night. Two days later, he told her, "You are an idiot. You are too picky. You are this and you are that." My God, in 48 hours everything changed. There was no reality in any of it. When she went to a psychoanalyst, the therapist told her, "During the first time he wanted you. By the second time he didn't. Don't be confused." This type of game, and the pain it creates, has become usual.

We habitually spin lies in the name of truth. We have become accustomed to this as a fact and even admire it like marketing. This is how our mental games drop us. We fall from our own innocence and descend from our own elevation. We are very beautiful and creative people. We are made in the image of God. We have the fastest and the most wonderful power—our own mind. It can take us to God. It can take us to ourselves. It can take us deep into our self or far out into the universe. The mind is so sensitive it can go into any bird, take the feelings of the bird, and tell us all those feelings. When clean and open the mind can do anything that we want.

Sometimes you feel stuck. There is a kind of inertia. You can't feel you. And you can't get out of a feeling. A student asked me, "How can I get out of my feelings?"

I said, "First decide who is feeling in you. Is it Miss Depresso or is it Miss Kaur—the Princess of Consciousness in you? Who are you?"

She said, "I don't know. I am totally caught in my feelings."

I said, "How are you caught? Are you caught by someone else? Tell me the feelings. Show me. Give me the root."

She shook her head saying, "I can't, I can't, I can't."

When you lose your elevation and have no habit to listen to your consciousness, then it seems like you have no choice. You do not understand it because your mind is doing this to you. Your mind is not supposed to do anything to you. Your mind is supposed to do things for you. Now you are caught in the game of mind and ego. Between the two you can be stretched until nothing is left.

If we can remember this one little thing and take it to heart, then we can solve our problems a hundred percent. Just remember: the mind is given to us, we are not given to the mind. It is a simple thing. What did I say? Can you repeat it out loud and listen to your own words? If you can listen and hear the power of your own spoken word, your own committed language, and if it is remembered by you, it becomes you. Say it and listen to it consciously. That is the work of the mind. It should listen consciously and help you be surprisingly successful.

The art and science of using sound to imprint and awaken the mind is called *Naad* Yoga. I have taught its inner science and secrets publicly for the first time for everyone. At one time it used to be taught to sages and rulers and healers. Now it has to be taught again because there is so much pain coming from these mind games. We must tame the mind and make it our servant and friend. There is no better way than through the power of the word, the *naad* of the *shabd* and the projection of the consciousness.

The window of your mind can be cleared or fogged over by the words you use and how you use them. There is a gap between what you say in words and what you intend to communicate. That is why you are so often confused. That is why we have to learn to honestly talk with each other. That is why we need to learn to notice when our mind has split off with the ego and emotions. The only thing that is communicated and is heard as it is at the same time is the truth. That is a power of your mind. It can penetrate the subtlety and intention behind someone's words and it can project and fill yours with a truth beyond any fear or need.

In the spiritual world, the words of a teacher are very precise. The job of the spiritual teacher is to be a warning. A spiritual teacher is not your guide and your destiny-maker. The teacher knows what your destiny is. He knows who you are in consciousness, in spirit, and in circumstance. But the main job is to give you a flashing red light at the proper time to avoid an accident. That way a potential accident can be turned into a harmless incident, and you can go on your way, by your own grace and consciousness. That is authentically spiritual. It is just like when your car stalls on the freeway. You put a sign out or some flashing red lights. Why do you go to that trouble and expense? Because you don't want someone to hit the back of your car. We all have the capacity to keep going mentally, physically, and spiritually. That is the Will of God, that is our construction and that is the flow. We only grow corrupt because our mind has started guiding us rather than serving us.

Your soul gives you awareness and the language of love. Your mind gives you consciousness to sense all the differences and the lines drawn. The teacher warns you and helps keep your mind clear, so that you can be guided by the light of awareness and use the power of your consciousness. Your habit in words and concept is to divide everything. What is yours and what is mine? You never remember what is God's and what is divine.

I talked to some one this weekend. They said, "I am out of my mind today." It was the first time I had ever heard this from someone.

I said, "What does that mean? How can you be out of your mind?"

She said, "Well, nothing sinks in. I hear the words and have a lot of feelings, but they just go by."

I said, "I can hardly believe this. My god, you say nothing at all sinks in? My dear one, the capacity and the faculty of your mind is a supersensitivity so that everything sinks in right away."

She looked worried and asked, "What is wrong with me? What can I do about it?"

I spoke to her directly, "You have a huge fat ego pad between your mind and you. That is why nothing sinks in. It is a big thick pad. When your ego is involved this way, put it in your left hand and close your hand into a fist. Now keep that ego there." Whenever the ego serves you, your intelligence doesn't. When intelligence doesn't serve you, wisdom leaves as well. The ego lets you know only what is yours. It becomes deaf and insensitive to receive anything else.

The language beyond mind and ego is love. It is a sixth sense. It is called union or merger. Sometimes you accomplish it. The majority of people here get married and set up everything separately. They marry and prepare for divorce on the first day. They have separate accounts, separate beds, separate pillows, separate bathrooms, separate rules, and separate minds. In the end they are really separate worlds. That is how the ego divides everything in the name of security or in the name of possession or in the name of being individual. What individuality can there be if you do not know you? Individuality without you is just difference. Individuality with you is uniqueness. I visited someone, and I saw they had two night-lights in one house. One was green and one was red. I asked, "What is this? Why are there two night-lights?" He said, "My wife likes the red light at night and I like the green." I said, "God bless you and this marriage." That is all we see and all we accommodate. Differences in colors, differences in cars, differences in beds, differences in everything. Your mind takes each feeling of the ego and expands it, stretches it into a line that divides you. Then you say, "I love you." But you do not know what that is. It is just some biscuit that you eat. It is a pleasing taste for today. You don't know how to speak in *naad* from the heart, beyond all barriers and without a mental condition and negotiation. Speak just from grace, from trust, from love, from your reality. You make a mental statement based on reacting to and facing the immediate time. In that way you face the time, and you face the time, and you face the time, until finally the times face you. Since you started with zero and spoke with zero, now you have zero to carry you through the time.

I saw a couple who were real. Unfortunately the wife developed cancer and was dying. The husband was deeply in love with her. She was beautiful, and she was dying without a hope for recovery. When I talked to the husband, he smiled. He was very happy. Then his uncle came in the hospital room and said, "John."

He said, "Yes, Uncle."

Uncle said, "Ruth is dying, and you are sitting there with a smile. I heard you tell her that you are grateful, and I heard, 'We were together and now this is the last time. But I will meet you there soon. It is not a problem. I am with you.'" The uncle asked, "Aren't you sad?"

He said, "No."

The uncle said, "You don't even realize that your wife is dying."

The husband said, "Uncle, my wife is not dying. She is very clever and intelligent. She is just going home early. I have to follow her. I am giving her a good send off. She is so beautiful. Can't you see she is beautiful, she is intelligent, she is pure, and she is bright? I am a little down. I want to join her. But I have more chores to do, more karma to complete before my call comes. I am with her nonetheless, and she with me. I am not lonely."

That was a condition of love, of merger, and no barrier. The mind only served the relationship, the reality, and the dignity.

You have the ability and intelligence and consciousness. You are just scared. That is why you need to practice meditation, *naam simran* and *jappa* to cleanse the fear out of the mind. You can tune up your mind with a sacred tune of God, with the words of truth from the Guru that penetrate your heart. The maximum percentage of your brain you can use consciously is about five percent out of a hundred. But if you use only point three percent of your brain capacity consciously, intelligently, and without ego, everything will go smoothly. You are the master of your destiny. You are the leader of your day. You are the light of your life. You are nothing but a representation of God on this planet. That is the Will and decree, and that is God. In God you dwell, and God dwells in you. It is mental forgetfulness and your fears that close the window of the mind, so you do not see the beauty and reality of your self. That is what causes all these unwanted and unnecessary ego troubles.

Beloved God, be kind to us, bless us to remember Thee now and forever.
Give us the consciousness to live, the truth to rely on, and Thy grace to walk with.
May those who have come here in Thy name be blessed and
delightfully received in consciousness. Make their journey fruitful,
their listening graceful, and their life full of virtues so they can carry
Thy message into the world of today and tomorrow.
Sat Naam.

7 Speak with Committed Language

The greatest blunder that almost everyone makes is the feeling that you have to speak whatever is on your mind. That doesn't make sense. Your language becomes a loudspeaker and you sound like a squawking duck. The mind has automatic waves of thought and feelings from many sources. You are not meant to speak all of that. The mind is meant to know the truth. Train your mind to speak the truth in a committed language so it is beautiful and effective.

Language is our most powerful interface with the mind. It can exalt us or demean us. Mostly we use language by reflex and impulse. How should we use language to express our consciousness and increase our awareness? What happens when we do not? This talk challenges your concept and use of language in its relationship with your mind.

7

IN THE REALITY OF YOUR OWN STRUCTURE AND EXISTENCE, THE MIND is given to you to so you can act, express, and experience your self in this creation. Instead of training your mind and using its power, you have become a slave of the mind. Your only problem is the misbehavior of your own mind. Neither your body does anything wrong, nor your soul does anything wrong. It is very unfortunate when a human being cannot reach the Neutral Mind. When you cannot reach your Neutral Mind, you are reactive. You act as a beast instead of a human. I'm sorry to tell you this, but it is true. When you cannot reach the Neutral Mind, you never know what is right and what is wrong. You lack the clarity and certainty of your soul.

You are an intelligent person who knows everything, educates yourself, feeds yourself, decorates yourself, wears clothes, and accomplishes great things. But when you cannot speak with a committed language of consciousness, it is very degrading. You seem shallow and look like an idiot when someone asks you, "Did you really say this? Is that what you meant?" And you cannot say yes or no. When you waver and cannot say directly what is true or real, then you fall before your own self. You are belittled. How could you do this to your self? How could you act with so little scope, depth, or reality? Without the Neutral Mind, you protect yourself with diversions, manipulations, and lies. This game of lies catches up with you. When that happens, it brings an end to your personality. It brings an end to your psyche and your projection. It limits you and diminishes you from your trust and reliance on Infinity. It brings an end to the flow of your confidence. Whenever you lie it takes away a chunk from you that is called self-confidence. I don't mind your lies. It is not a personal problem for me. But it is a problem for you. Instead of lies, practice the art of committed language so you can tap the power and beauty of your mind.

Committed language is very special. It is an innate capacity we all have. Committed language is when you speak directly, with your heart, with all parts of your mind supporting what you say. It means you speak from the Neutral Mind, having processed the thought with all three Functional Minds. Your self is committed to the impact of your words unto Infinity. If you listened to those words after 100 years, you would still approve the statement. When you hear the words, they are full of spirit and not just mechanical or intellectual. They are filled with you, with your purpose, with the reality of you as a creative being. Committed language is direct, truthful, and spoken from your heart with full awareness of the other person, your roles, and obligations.

Normally you do not speak with committed language. The result is your love is not committed, your compassion is not committed, and your relationships are not committed. Uncommitted relationships are very painful. There is fear, no trust, unconscious anger, and mistake after mistake. To get rid of that pain, you drink. You drink so much you can become an alcoholic. If you don't drink, you find some other drugs. You become a drug addict. You do all kinds of other weird things and damaging habits to avoid the pain. All these negative habits that belittle and subject your life are just tactics to cover over one great pain: your own hollowness. You try to bury the shallowness you feel. You have no depth because you are not committed. Without commitment in your language and actions you feel that you do not know what is going on. You are unsure and lack control. You react by feeling irritation and anger. Then you find lots of ways to let that anger out. One of the worst and most common ways is to harm yourself by lying.

Some people believe they are very clever. They are so clever that they think they can play games, they can lie, they can outsmart their own hollowness and suffer no reaction from all the lies they weave. They are beautiful, wonderful people. I don't have any trouble with them. They are a certain experience and style of life. But I know, with that belief, they shall be shallow and hollow forever. When you lie you think you can get away from something. You think you can save yourself and harm somebody else. You have the choice to lie for the rest of your life. But each time you lie, you lose a piece of your self-confidence.

A lie is nothing but a habit. It takes away confidence and it comes from a lack of confidence. It is a vicious circle of insecurity and pain. If you don't want to say something, don't! You do not have to lie. Instead just speak up, "I don't want to say it." It takes courage to say, "I don't want to say it." But that courage builds you. It lets you speak directly from your own depth. Instead when you feel cornered you say, "I don't know." This is a lie. You do know. It is a common lie which we all practice. Everybody knows where they are and why they are what they are. It is a fundamental sensitivity each of us has.

We lack a simple, clear analysis of why people lie so much when it harms them and limits them. To start just think, "What is a lie?" It is anything spoken with uncommitted language. Any word spoken under fear in which your personality is not clear is a lie. Lying is not a sin. Lying is a habit. It is a damaging habit, but just a habit like any other habit.

Why do people lie? They lie because they cannot love. Instead of loving and giving love, they seek to be loved. They want validation. They act like little beggars who need the good will of the entire world. They do not rely on the goodwill of God and validate themselves.

Do not seek anything from people. Give love instead, and rely on God. But remember, God is not different than your own soul. There is no such thing as God separate from you. God is in your own soul, and that soul goes through every molecule, every atom of you. Now an average person has over ten trillion cells. All those cells and the projection of the soul changes and renews itself every 72 hours. So you are constantly renewed and given new energy to make choices. If you lied yesterday, and you lied today, but you don't lie tomorrow, you will be all right. You can rewrite your projection and start to use the power of committed language in your life. This is my main point. It is very ineffective for you to live in falsehood and lies. You will not know who you are or what you are doing, and you will become dependent on something or someone.

When you don't have the habit to speak directly with committed language, you will create emotional diversions from your own bad feelings. I was sitting in the Albuquerque Airport. I was talking to a mother about her son. She said, "I want my son to come home and stay with me instead of being at school." I said, "Yes, you are his mother and you want your son. But ask yourself and answer honestly, can you handle him?" She looked at me and said, "I don't know." Can you believe this answer? She wants him but she knows she cannot handle the situation. But she says she doesn't know. So, I said, "Why don't you try it for a while and check it out carefully. If you find you can handle him, then it is fine with us. If not, then let him go." She did not know what to do with her loneliness.

This kind of drama is an emotional diversion tactic Sometimes you may feel very lonely. You feel it inside your self. You want to know why you are lonely. You search for the cause. What is the reason? Then you divert your mind. You find a friend or a boyfriend, and you go to a party or put on a party yourself. Anything to involve your mind and divert your attention from the bad feelings. The problem is that you can divert your mind from reality temporarily, but you can never ignore reality. It haunts you. It haunts you because everything is a reality. It is just as the spiritual insight proclaims: God is everywhere.

ਇਹੁ ਜਗੁ ਸਚੈ ਕੀ ਹੈ ਕੋਠੜੀ ਸਚੇ ਕਾ ਵਿਚਿ ਵਾਸੁ

Eh jag sachai kee hai kotharee sachay kaa vich vaas

- Guru Nanak, *Siri Guru Granth Sahib*, page 463

The world is the True Lord's chamber. Within it the True One resides.

This whole world is truth and only truth dwells in it. Lies don't. Therefore, the truth will continue to haunt you, and the lies will evaporate. Not only will the lies evaporate, they will evaporate you! Somewhere along the cycle of the lying and the lies to support the lying, you are caught lying. And that is it. You are caught being phony, being jealous, and being belittled. Caught, caught, caught, caught.

And one day, you are just cut. Your lies have cut you off from your self and from reality. They have squandered the power and potential of your mind. Once you are cut out, how can you go back? Where is there to go? You have lied to your self so much you do not know where you have come from. You have lied to your self to not look at or know where you are going. You are scared. That is why you call death "going home to God," and yet you are afraid of it. Can you understand this? Your lies have made you scared. You even fear the Unknown, which has created and nurtured you. When you separated from God and came into the human form, you were in pain. You came to a very unknown place called the planet Earth. You came to unknown people called parents. You came to unknown environments and food. First your mother nursed you and then you nursed yourself. You grew and then you became passionate to know. You wanted experience and to consciously know. If you guide that passionate self to become the compassionate self, committed and vast, and then experience God, then life is beautiful. It is so simple. Then your mind acts fearlessly with kindness and compassion to express you.

The greatest blunder I have seen that almost everyone makes is to just speak their mind. It doesn't make any sense. They sound like the squawking ducks in a pond. The mind is not meant to be spoken. The mind is mostly automatic waves of thoughts and sensations from many sources. The mind is meant to know the truth. Know your own mind and use it to speak the truth. Train your mind to speak the truth in a committed language, so it is beautiful and effective. If you speak whatever the mind pushes forward, you won't make any sense. It will just be duck language.

Who do you think you are? You are not your mind, nor do you belong to the mind. The mind is yours. If the mind is yours, where do you apply the control to direct it? Where do you apply the analytic mind to understand what you have done? That is the use of committed language—where the self is projected in its totality without limit. Instead, you just speak your fears, your anger, your hatred, and your ignorance. You speak your passions and your lust. If that is not enough then you write it. If that is not enough, you imagine, fantasize, and counter-imagine until you are spaced out or depressed.

To understand how to use your mind and break the web of lies, you must grasp the nature of committed language. Your common observations and expressions are not realities, and Infinity itself cannot be spoken. This is the normal situation. And there are so many Infinities in our experience. God is Infinity. Love is Infinity. Commitment is Infinity. In every facet of our life we have the potential for the Infinity of our projection. Projecting with Infinity in our speech is the base of committed language.

In old Vedic language the Infinity of your projection is called *patantar*. *Patantar* is when this trinity of body, mind, and soul all project towards Infinity. *Pa* means the total sum of *tantar*. *Tantar* means length and breadth. It is a two word sound—*pa-tantar*. Together the sounds make the word *patantar* which means our total projection towards Infinity. We use this concept when we say about a very wise person, *Baraa patantar hai*. It means that person's projection is great. It is within the reach of Infinity, and Infinity is within the reach of his projection.

Let's practice speaking with this projection. How do you say, "I am your friend" in a committed language? You meet and just say, "Hey friend!" That is all. In "*naad* language" it has two strokes to its impact. "Hey" is the projection and "friend!" is the confirmation. Committed language comes from the heart. Language which comes not from the heart but from the head is nothing but a bunch of lies. When the head is subject to the heart you are in ecstasy with the conscious self. When the heart is subject to the head it is too ugly to even speak about.

Now say, using committed language, "You are very beautiful." Try it yourself first. In a committed language it would be, "Wow, hey you." This basic phrase has a triple stroke to its impact and accent. "Wow" is the projection. "Hey" expands the projection. "You" is the personal penetration. This triple stroke commands the mind from the heart and reaches the Neutral Mind.

Here is one last example. Committed language captures the Negative and Positive Minds and uses the Neutral Mind. All three are balanced. If you want to give your promise and make a commitment and you say, "Don't worry," you have not completed your Projection. You are not well defined within your promise. Any confirmed commitment must contain both polarities. When you speak it, you speak to both sides of the coin—negative and positive. Instead of saying to someone, "I have told you the truth," you must qualify it in committed language. Say, "This is the truth, take it or leave it." That is committed language. You expressed that you are not worried because there is nothing but truth, and you know the guy has no choice. You say, "Take it or leave it. It is up to you. Don't bother about me." Normally people who speak truth say something like, "Don't believe me. Experience it." They do not sell themselves to you. When you speak truth you don't need to sell anything. It is already sold. It is ever-living. It will never go anywhere.

We who have practiced life consciously know this language of truth. I can also read auras. God has not given me the same eyes that he has given to you. All these things tell me what you are saying and how much truth there is in what you say. It is very fascinating to watch the rainbow of auric colors and see someone talking and lying and still trying to express and communicate. It shows one lesson very clearly: you can not take a garden hose and use it to penetrate through a bulletproof wall. It doesn't work. That hose is just like your lies. Lies don't work at all. They cannot penetrate to the heart, and they cannot take your projection to Infinity beyond time. They serve only to satisfy your ego. Your heart, your soul, and the reality in others are not satisfied. Sometimes people will listen to you, even with your lies, and out of compassion they will pretend with you. Later on they realize you are a liar, and then they abuse you. So, it is totally ridiculous to use lies. Talk from your heart. Master the art of committed language, and use your mind to project to the Infinity in every facet of your life.

You all want to be successful. What should your profile be like to be successful? When you want to be successful and very convincing, just feel truth in your heart. Be sure. Be confident. Feel that truth in your heart, then speak that truth from the heart. Don't try to run it around or manipulate it with your brain or head.

There is a secret to courageousness. There has to be a base from which you speak, a foundation in committed language within you. If your base is your ego and personality, you can fall flat. If your base is only personal experience, you will be very limited. If you form a base on the Guru's words, you can never be defeated. You will have invincibility in your spirit. The Guru's words in the *Siri Guru Granth Sahib* are the perfect committed language where the heart commands the mind to serve Infinity. Once those incantations of the Infinite are in your heart, the truth will always seem sweet and victory in life will be yours.

Sat Naam.

8 Enrich Your Mind

Your mind is designed as a preparatory system to guide and aid your life. It is a power to gather your resources and shape your behavior. You can refine the mind, its Facets, and all its combinations. Then you can act effectively in your Executive Mind, Creative Mind, Applied Mind, and hundreds of others. But you must train and refine the mind to give you those Functional Minds that serve you and your soul.

The mind forms patterns based on habits. Those habits are woven from our attention and from our thoughts. To break the shackles of low thoughts and habits, we have the ability to dwell in the vastness of our soul. By enriching and refining the mind and its Facets, we form a relationship within us that supports our projection to lead and contribute to the world.

8

YOU HAVE FASHIONS AND FACULTIES IN YOUR MIND. YOUR FASHION is how you decide to look, act, and be; how you want to project your self into the world. You can be a person of spirit, a person of great mental intellect, a person of brute force, a healer, or a leader. Your faculties are the functions, aspects and projections that give you abilities. To excel and enjoy life you need to enrich your mind. You must blend and use different combinations of your mental facets to support you and your intentions. When your faculties support your mental fashion and your fashion supports you, you become effective and share a legacy that inspires others.

We have discussed three major faculties of your mind: Negative, Positive, and Neutral. Each has its own function and nature. They combine in different ways to support or to block various mental projections. The Negative Mind is your first and fastest. It interacts with your thoughts first. It is a protector developed to preserve your life. It can give you a powerful self-understanding and detailed critiques of your actions. It can tell you what is wrong, what might be harmful, and it can locate problems to be solved.

The Positive Mind seeks out what is useful and what can be of benefit. It is results oriented and proposes many solutions and possible avenues of action.

Then you have the Neutral Mind. It is a subtle mind that looks at all positive and negative Facets, assesses, and finds the depths and implications.

Three minds are very essential for excellence in your life: the Applied Mind, Creative Mind, and the Executive Mind. Each is unique in its particular combination of faculties and Facets. The Applied Mind seeks out the Positive Mind's solutions, but limits them to what is directly applicable to your goal. In this way it is strong, extremely simple, and achieves results quickly. It also prevents overloading that can occur if the Positive Mind spins off on its own freely. A refined Applied Mind is a great asset to accomplish much in your life. If you have converted part of your Positive Mind to the Applied Mind, then the thoughts released by the Negative Mind go to the Positive Mind. The Negative Mind is substituted by a positive attitude, and the Applied Mind solves its problems. You cannot be depressed or blocked. Besides the Applied Mind you have a subtle and very powerful mind—the Creative Mind. It is a sweet little thing. Its source is so potent it gives you a direct intuition. It is original and unique.

With all these minds you have another—the Executive Mind. It is a Projective Mind. It moves actions and resources. A lot of people fail because they can't or won't decide things. They hesitate and lose the timing or become doubtful and lose the leadership. They will discuss things, shuffle papers, and plan. The Executive Mind decides in seconds. When you have difficult decisions, like a surgeon dealing with life and death, this mind is essential.

Your mind is designed as a preparatory system to guide and aid your life. It is a power to gather your resources and shape your behavior. You can refine the mind, its Facets, and all its combinations. Then you can act effectively in your Executive Mind, Creative Mind, Applied Mind, and hundreds of others. But you must train and refine the mind to give you those Functional Minds that serve you and your soul.

The greatest thing you can do is rise in the early morning and do a *sadhana*—a practice to energize the body and refine your mind. Most of us rebel and go crazy rather than get up early. There are two special time zones, when you have to enrich your mind: one in the morning, from 4 a.m. to 8 a.m., and one in the evening, from 4 p.m. to 8 p.m. These are natural moments that have a tide of energy within you and without. The sun and Earth have a special relationship and angle at those times that affect your mind and your energy.

Have you seen all these people who drink, who search for a partner, and who look for drugs? They start the search in earnest, or have the urge to do it, after 4 p.m. Why do they need drink? Why do people feel they need to take drugs? Do they drink to relax? No. So why do they drink? They do all that out of an instinct to seek stimulation. At those times their biorhythm has gone down, and they feel irritated. They cannot exist like that and have to have a change. Eating a lot of meat just adds to the body's uric acid that acts as a very powerful stimulant, though it is a harmful force. And adding liquor damages the liver, but it still feels like a stimulant. Without stimulation at that time people are angry. They act lousy, lazy, and leery. Why? What is behind this phenomenon? The root cause is that your basic biorhythm of energy, your mental projection and strategy are not reflected in a unisonness of character. Those zones are natural times that shift your energy level, your mental projection, and your performance. That is the time you must direct the mind, refine it, and create a consolidated unisonness of character and projection.

Why won't you use that time? Why not rise in the twilight of early morning and prepare yourself? You sense the change in energy, why not elevate yourself and refine your mind and its faculties? You don't even get up just to face a problem that bothers you. The fact is, you are a part of this cosmos and the cosmos is part of you. You open your eyes to face the universe and all of its problems! And you do not want to accept this. You are too insecure to face this reality. You revert, invert, and divert your mind to not look. When you open your eyes, don't open them to see how to be rich. Open your eyes to be able to make people rich. Don't open your eyes to become wise or gather knowledge. Open your eyes to make other people wise. Become vast and remember that you are a part of this entire cosmos. It's a cosmos that should be served by you and the legacy of your wisdom, love, affection, sweetness, kindness, and your compassion and caring. Train your mind to relate to your totality and to act without fear.

Your mind vibrates and will deliver your thoughts. It has a mechanism. The *shushmanaa,* the central channel of the spine, connects to the *shashaaraa,* the crown chakra. Each projected thought will vibrate a thousand in return, and those go to the cosmos like an indelible record. For each negative thought, you have to face one thousand negative thoughts. For one negative action, you'll have to face the impact of one thousand negative actions. But you don't know your mind and its Facets. The result is someone is rude to somebody. Someone doubts and mistrusts somebody.

Why? For each disrespect, you'll in turn not be respected. This lack of grace, mistrust, and abuse is a habit. You did not train your mind to realize you are here for only a few years and have a chance to serve, touch, and leave a legacy for all. God has trusted you and respected you enough to give you this body and to put two of you together in this huge world. What is there to trust or not trust?

Will you live isolated, mistrusting, and small? It is against your nature. Problem is not whether you will live and how rich you can be. The problem is how much impact you have, how many legacies you leave, how much grace you show, and how much vastness you experience. Will you die like a little worm, burrowed in the earth, where no one, not even a grandchild, will remember you and have thanks? That is a choice. That is why you encounter the mind. That is why you rise in the twilight to become a huge light!

A human who by God's Grace has a face, but who cannot or will not face all of life, is the worst of all incarnations on this Earth. Everything, every animal, both the hunter and the hunted, communicate with each other, except humans. It is most shocking. It's very surprising. Have you seen two rams fighting in the mountains? Everyone knows they are fighting, and the best one will survive. There's no sneakiness in it. If as a human you train your mind to make every action sneaky, you will not have a face and live with your grace. If someone calls, "Oh, tell her I'm not home, not available." Thank God, with modern answering machines you don't have to face anyone at all. This pattern of fear and lack of mental refinement is called Diagonal Self-destruction. It is a mental phenomenon. You get on a pedestal, a status with face, and you act to split it right through, diagonally down. Once you do this you will never, ever rise again. That's the way this world is. That's how the world of the mind works.

Just open your eyes, train your mind, and do your actions. Your actions will tell you how near or far you are from God. Be direct and face up to your own Infinite vastness. Have vastness as an attitude. Don't sneak, hide, and avoid the crown of soul and body God gave you. Anyone who has no sense or attitude of vastness, no mental refinement to see the vastness will at any moment, for no reason, prostitute his own grace, and lose life, leadership, and legacy.

When you acknowledge your vastness, you have manners. Your mind supports your projection. The evidence of that is love. Love is the living power of Infinity. Where there's a love, there's no question. Where there's a question, there's no love. It is beyond your mental corruptions and calculations. If you say, "I love you," then that's it. Stop there, the matter ends. But you don't love. Oh, yes, you can have sexual, sensual love and public, social love. You do have the love of money, the love of this thing and that thing. You love to collect things. You have so many loves. But what about love pure and simple, vast and clear? You can not even sense that you are the most deceitful, disgusting human beings when you use the word "love" for a bait on a hook. Even animals don't do that. At least they are pure, with strong passions that are straightforward and simple.

That is where your curse is. Your mind locks into its Negative Mind, all the way. It is not linked nor refined. Then by reflex you compete, compare, and you become confused. You ignore your real impact and nature and you act rude, crude, and obnoxious. You act without self-control, without self-grace, and with no self-esteem. You can have lot of degrees, tons of money, astounding muscles, and be very sharp and quick. You may be superhuman in all these respects, but you will not have superior graceful manners because you are still mentally defunct. If you have not established some vastness in your attitude, then your habits and facets, your fears and pettiness will betray you.

An old saying assures us that if you put a dog on a throne and a crown on its head, the moment he gets a chance, he will go lick the grinding wheel. He can't help it. It's the habit of a dog, just as your corruptions are habits of your mind and its Facets. If your mind is crude and attached to the Earth and abandoned by you at the twilight times, then it doesn't matter how many buildings and how many banks you have. With all your billions, you still will eat only two *chapatis* [a flatbread]. And if you didn't care for your teeth and you don't chew well, you will still have a stomach problem.

What is the cure? The protection? This is the secret of the mind enriched by vastness and the secret power of the devotee who trained the mind. The mental world within you has to be one world in unison. All 81 Facets of the mind must reach to the best—not good, not better—to the *best*. Then the three Minds—Negative, Positive, and Neutral—act on that to serve you to be the best. And over all those minds there is your awareness that controls and supervises the mind. It assesses if it happens to be the best, real, and whole. Finally, you can surrender your mind to your spirit. When you will surrender your mind to your soul, then the soul will make God surrender to you. Don't react in doubt, guilt, or insecurity. This is a truth. The Bhagats said it this way:

ਮੇਰੀ ਬਾਂਧੀ ਭਗਤੁ ਛਡਾਵੈ ਬਾਂਧੈ ਭਗਤੁ ਨ ਛੂਟੈ ਮੋਹਿ

Mayree baandhee bhagat chadhaavai, baandhai bhagat na chutai mo-eh

-Namdev, *Siri Guru Granth Sahib*, page 1252

A devotee can release anyone from My bondage,

but I cannot release anyone from his.

If the Infinite wants something, a devotee can change it. But if a devotee says something, then God cannot undo it. The devotee is merged in that vastness, relies on it, and has no barrier of ego between the two. So the One must stand for the one. Each thought and act stirs the universe and many subtleties occur. They seem like mysteries, but they are masteries.

Once a *sadhu*, a wandering holy man, had absolutely nothing to cover his body except a little piece of cloth to put over his private organ. He was walking and somebody saw him. He stopped and said to him, "Hey, *Sadhu*, this is lunch time. Will you walk with me to my house and let us feed you?"

He replied, "Okay." The *sadhu* came. He was served and fed well.

The wife of the house came in. She said, "Hey, *Sadhu*, you don't have any clothes on your body. If I give you these clothes, will you wear them?"

He said, "Fine."

Then the son came home. "You must have shoes. I have these beautiful wooden shoes. Take them for your journey."

He said, "Okay."

Just as he was going, they all said, "You are a holy man. You have come to our house. You cannot go empty handed. Here are one hundred and one rupees. Please accept them."

"Okay," he said, and left.

Everyone thought, "I wonder who he is? Why did he come this way?"

The father said, "When I saw him, I had a feeling. I had to bring him."

"We had a feeling, too. We respected him. We felt we should serve him."

That night as they slept, gangsters and ruffians came to loot the village. Their habit was to shoot guns and make a lot of noise. Five or six of them came on top of their roof. They heard a great racket and gunfire. Six bodies fell right from the skylight opening used for ventilation. The family was saved. No one was injured. In the morning, the police came. They took away those six bodies. The family was grateful and also a little upset.

Three days later a man walked by. He looked like a wise man and a pundit. The father from that house stopped him and told him, "I have a problem."

The pundit said, "What is it?"

He said, "Those bandits came and shot each other right on my roof. It is their habit to always shoot the guns. How could it happen that they shot each other and all fell dead?"

The pundit asked, "Do you believe in the words of Guru Nanak?"

He said, "Yes."

Then the pundit recited,

ਕਰਮੀ ਆਵੈ ਕਪੜਾ ਨਦਰੀ ਮੋਖੁ ਦੁਆਰੁ
Karmee aavay kaparaa nadaree mokh duaar
   -Guru Nanak, *Siri Guru Granth Sahib*, page 2 (4th *pauree* of *Japji Sahib*)
Each mortal obtains a human body as the result of good deeds,
and reaches the gate of salvation by God's kind look.

He asked, "What did you do in the morning? God put a shield over your actions and redemption came to you through His sight."

He said, "We did nothing special. We did bring an old *sadhu* to the house and clothed and fed him."

The pundit smiled and said, "That's it. One noble action makes God give back one hundred thousand noble actions to cover you. It's a law."

Your mind is not a joke. This mind of yours is a part of the Master Mind, the Universal Mind. That Master Mind is the custodian of the Almighty's force. In the Almighty's force, you are also a force. What can you do? Who are you? What is your concept? If you are not intermingled with that vastness, if you have not absolutely surrendered yourself into the Totality of this existence-life, then you will feel very independent, lonely, confused, and live a cursed life. You will have no following, no students, no trail of impact, and no tale for a legacy. You will be just one person—born, and died; that's it. You never came out. Your ego, fears, and commotions are a cocoon, you will never hatch, blossom, and be beautiful.

That cocoon is woven from your habits—your mental patterns. You are such a slave of your habits, that you can never free yourself. You are so bound and stitched into your neuroses, you will never feel free. Your judgement will be biased; your words will be biased; your social relationships will be biased; your projection will be biased; and your living will be biased. Your facets and reactions will limit you. The tragedy is that everybody knows it, except you who thinks it is hidden. It is only the egomaniac who doesn't know. Every one else in every realm of consciousness does know.

Without vastness and an enriched mind, you entangle in earth and try to have everything and end up with nothing. Husbands fight with wives. Father fights with the children. Children fight with the mother. There's no familiarity, no capacity of connection. You do not develop anything and there is no depth.

Where is your kindness, tolerance, compassion, and humility? You come, you live, you die. Dust to dust. Have you heard the priest say that? "Heavenly Father, we go dust unto dust." You will never hear the priest say, "Heavenly Father, our dust is going to the heavens." He can't say it. And he doesn't know how to make it. The one power and gift you have from the Almighty is the mind. When the mind is enriched, when the mind has all the 81 Facets together, that mind which has all the projections together is capable of Infinity. Mind is the only power you have which is positive, and can be definitely finite or definitely positively Infinite. It can reach both ends of the pendulum.

When you enrich your mind you can break the slavery of low habits and ego. You can act as part of the entire cosmos and learn to elevate and to let go. Everything you hold onto, that you feel you possess, that is not a gift creates a karma, a debt. What is it you can give in life? When your mind is subtle, what can you give? You can give money, advice, a job, and many things. But that giving in itself is worthless if it has expectation with it. The only thing you can truly give someone is forgiveness. For the sake of giving, forgive. If you have an iota of refined mind, forgive, and forget it. Act from your grace, manners, and awareness, and trust the hand of God. You can not understand and master the mind without this knowledge of yourself, your reality, and your spirit.

There's a beautiful story about Guru Gobind Singh, the Tenth Guru of the Sikhs, that shows the reality of karma, the power of the mind, and the beautiful sophistication of dharma. There was a businessman who was also a very good devotee. He had succeeded in a great business venture. His big trade fleet produced a profit of a hundred thousand fold. He went to the ruler of that area, a Muslim Nawab. He told him, "I have brought all these presents for you." The ruler was very happy and said, "My friend, you always give me so many presents and so much love. Tell me honestly what I can do for you. Tell me and I'll do it."

He said, "I'm a businessman but I have a Guru, Guru Gobind Singh. I want to present him with the best swords, shields, arrows, and horses. They should be even better than your own best."

The ruler said, "Do you know how much money you are talking about?"

The merchant said, "Yes. I can give it to you in advance now."

The ruler said, "No, that's not the deal. I'll get you everything you can imagine. It will be the best of the best. But five percent of it shall be for my efforts."

He said, "Fine. Done."

It took six months. Everything was forged and created as the strongest, best, and most artistic. The merchant took many carts loaded with everything. He came to see Guru Gobind Singh. He went as a real devotee with humility, head bowed, and arms outstretched. He asked for permission to stay a month or two and enjoy the company of the Lord. The list of gifts was given to the Guru who said, "They should be put in the storeroom." When the merchant opened his eyes to see the Guru's face, he witnessed something funny. The Guru had a pigeon in his hand and a wild hawk was tearing the flesh from it as the Guru sat. That shocked him. Seized by feelings, he immediately said, "I must be permitted to go very soon. I won't stay the two months you graciously granted me."

The Guru said, "So be it."

As the merchant left and passed the gate, Guru called to Bhai Daya Singh, "Bring this guy back."

When he returned the Guru said, "Do you have doubt about something?"

The merchant said, "No, Sir, no, no my Lord."

The Guru said, "But there must be something. You planned to stay two months and now you can't stay even one day? Speak directly."

He said, "My Lord, your hawk is always well fed. It needs nothing. And this is a wild hawk torturing this poor pigeon. A hawk can hunt the pigeon and do it, that's natural. But you are helping and tearing this little meat and muscle and feeding the hawk yourself. That does shock me. Now, I've no doubt you must do it for some purpose."

The merchant spoke with emotion and duality. He thought something had gone wrong. But he said, "Lord, whatever you are doing is perfect. You know all. You are Omniscient, Omnipotent, but I just had this thought."

The Guru said, "Why don't you ask these two birds what the problem is?"

He replied, "My Lord, how can the hawk and pigeon speak?

The Guru said, "Both are alive yet. If you just ask them, they will answer you."

The man gathered his devotional feelings and bowed with palms together toward the birds. He said, "Oh, hawk and pigeon, please solve my problem."

Both spoke with one voice, "There's no problem to solve. Who the hell are you?"

He said, "Just tell me what is going on?"

The birds said, "We'll tell you what is going on. I used to be Sikh So-and-So, and he was Sikh Such-and-Such. I went to him and asked him, 'Give me some money on loan.' We both witnessed it and then put the Guru as a witness to it. The Guru was our Guarantor. Then Such-and-Such died. I decided not to return that money to his family. Then I died. Today I'm a pigeon and he's a hawk. He wants my meat to clear the debt. I tried my best to escape but he caught me. I requested, 'Take me to the Guru because we agreed the Guru is the Guarantor. In his presence we'll ask him to return that loan of mine."

They said, "We are just settling the account. Why are you so upset? What makes you so disturbed?"

The merchant said, "But you are alive and life is sacred."

They said, "Life? What about all those lies which we did? We have to deal with those, too, or how can we be free?"

They were more concerned for their awareness and karmas than just holding life. When karmas remain so do you. Karma has to become dharma. Dharma is where the account is cleared. It is where your discipline and commitments make you positive and graceful. Then you break out of your cocoon and become a leader, elevate all and leave a legacy. That ability to turn negative into positive, to support all your actions with your facets and manners is the result of meditation. It comes with the refined mind. It is what develops through *sadhana* and *aradhana*. Through *jappa* and discipline.

When you stay in your own ego, the other person will find that you are only for your self. You are empty and have no world. These types of people have minds which are very negative, fearful, and cannot think positive, let alone neutral. This universe, this life, this body, and you are not a curse and not a mistake. By the Will of God you are in that image and have earned a life of grace, glory, and greatness. That is what you are born for. We only forget sometimes to be vast. We become too near and personal and have contempt for teachings, teacher, and the world. Just forgive, excel, and lead with grace to leave a legacy of kindness and compassion.

Give this prayer with me: God, give me the vastness, the courage so I can be kind. Give me the strength so that I can serve. Give me the wisdom so I can be positive. Give me the nature so that I can be compassionate. I ask Thee in Thy Name to uplift me my soul so I can serve all in Thy Name.
Sat Naam.

9 Select Your Path

Many people believe that the spiritual path is difficult and the neurotic path is easy. Students profess it and even some teachers encourage this idea. I have never agreed to it nor am I willing to agree to it now. It takes the same effort and energy to walk either path. The difficulty lies in the nature of the mind and how it grasps things and becomes entranced by feelings and sensations. The problem lies in being subject to time rather than being one step ahead of time.

We often fight the wrong battle. We do not identify the real problem. The problem is not the spiritual path. It is the way we react to immediate feelings rather than to the things that will be with us through time and beyond time. We make sense of our soul, remote or close, according to how we handle our mind. Direct the mind with immediate sensations and convoluted negotiations, and we create neurosis and confusion. Direct it with the power of an Infinite word, words of truth, and we will excel with clarity, kindness, and love.

9

I have heard repeatedly that many people believe that the spiritual path is difficult and the neurotic path is easy. Students profess it, and even some teachers encourage this idea. I have never agreed to it, nor am I willing to agree to it now. This is a life choice we must all make. If you do not understand the mind and its reactions, your first chosen step will be wrong, and your whole progress will be painful. It takes the same effort and energy to walk either path. The difficulty lies in the nature of the mind and how it grasps things and becomes entranced by feelings and sensations. The problem lies in being subject to time rather than being one step ahead of time.

To understand the situation, it is not necessary to become complicated. If we take a direct approach, and if we can understand the simplicity and beauty of God, then we can realize who we are. We can realize where we are at and where the energy we call life is at. Then we can establish a relationship to life and to our choices. The total sum of this life and this Earth, of this planet, this cosmos, and this space is nothing but energy. Call it any kind of theory you want, this life is constructed so that the energy of existence is transferred into matter. That matter can also be transferred into energy. Whatever the details of your theory, somehow that essential energy created matter and that matter sustains us through the energy! Life is about that balance and exchange of energy.

Whatever path we take in life, the requirement of life is the same. For a spiritual path it takes X amount of discipline of the mind and body. To accomplish that discipline takes Y amount of energy. For a neurotic path it also takes X amount of discipline of the mind and body. To accomplish those habits and training also takes Y amount of energy. Whether you decide to be a thief or a saint, you must still meditate to direct your mind, direct your energy and actions. Each has its own habits and challenges. It takes the same energy, the same amount of meditation to become a confirmed thief as a confirmed saint. The same energy must be directed!

If it does not take more energy then what is the difficulty? Why do we have the impression that one is easier than the other? If they are equal, why aren't all people spiritual? There are churches, synagogues, temples, and gurdwaras everywhere—teachings are available. What is the problem?

The answer is very simple. The Facets and Aspects of the mind react to the short-term stronger than to the long-term. The ego of the mind attaches to immediate impressions. It enjoys the entanglement, the struggle for control, and the intensity and drama—regardless of whether the sensation is pleasant, or painful. The reaction to become entranced and distracted from the long run is automatic in the Facets and momentum of the mind[1]. The spiritual path is a long haul. It is vast, subtle, and refined. The neurotic path is immediate, reactive, right there. It is tangible, and automatically physically expressed. You feel each of your neuroses and commotions through the physical upset and stimulation. Without any sensitivity, you can feel your traumas and dramas. You easily feel your depression and aggression. You go after immediate feelings. And there are so many feelings. Your mind becomes heavy and dense with those feelings. Everything else fades to the background. Your soul and you become more and more remote. Your soul, your most intimate friend, seems very remote in time. Then acting by commitment and grace becomes remote in space. Then you lose face and grace and ultimately the race! There is only one simple fact: On the spiritual path you have to pass through your mind, your power in experience, to reach the soul. But mind is not bound in time and space. So you must create a focus, an identity, a sensitivity to be beyond time and beyond the challenge of space. Then the soul is always immediate and present. It gives you a flow and makes your presence glow.

The Guru puts the situation in a single line:

ਮਨਿ ਵਿਧ ਚਾਣਨ ਵੇਖਿਆ
Man vidh chaanan vaykhiaa

Man means the mind. *Vidh* means to make a hole, like when you punch a hole in the earlobe to put in earrings. *Man vidh* is a very beautiful phrase. It means you penetrate through the mind and make a hole in it, like a pearl, or a bead. That is a procedure. A condition to walk the path, *man vidh*. Then the Guru completes it: *Man vidh chaanan vaykhiaa. Chaanan* is the light, the Infinite reality. *Vaykhiaa* is to see. So, you must go through the mind, penetrate it, and through that hole see the light beyond. That is what soul is. That is also what God is. That vision takes you beyond your reactions and carries you for the long run to Infinity.

The mind is like a camel. Have you ever gone on a camel ride? If you are not an expert you will tear your skin and pull your muscles and legs along with every other part. To ride the camel successfully you have a special way to sit on it, and a special way of synchronizing with its motion. And if you are very lucky you have a nail through its nose so you can direct it. Then it can carry you over endless deserts. If on one day that nail is gone; you will remember that day well! The camel, by nature, knows all kinds of tricks to throw you. It loves to do it. Then, after you fall hard from about ten feet, the camel has a very effective policy. It sits on the ex-rider and relentlessly grinds it and finally kills it. Now, this is exactly what the mind does to you. You need to punch the hole and conquer the mind, ride it in synchrony to your path.

The mind is supposed to be your power, your instrument, and your projection. It can tell you where you are and what is going on. But that very mind becomes your enemy and it kills you. It brings your downfall. It was given to you to connect you to God, and to help you express and experience you. How can you put that nail in? How can you create the hole in the mind and see the beacon of the soul's light?

One way comes from the basic theory that everybody has a destiny. Destiny is your highest actions and consciousness in this life. It holds your sense of mission and purpose. One procedure to tap that inner compass of destiny is to get a spiritual name, a name according to your destiny. These days this is not a common technique. We don't realize the power of the word and the gift of destiny. We pick up any nickname. We do not calculate its impact and effect on that soul. Actually, when a child is given a name, the first thing he has to be told is what his destiny is. Why does he have this name? Names given according to feelings will take you to those feelings. Names given by destiny will take you to the destiny. It is just a meditation that everyone repeats for you. When you think of that person and repeat a name that calls on the destiny in them, you pray for that person and that person is blessed each time.

The destiny-name is the first step you can take to go to the destiny. Without a name there is nothing. Imagine that you are dropped in the middle of America and told, "Go and find the city of your destiny." Where do you start? Which city are you searching for? You can visit a thousand cities and still not know whether your destiny city is San Francisco, or Los Angeles. A destiny name gives you a sense of your identity beyond circumstance, distraction, and immediate feelings.

I experienced its power myself. When I touched my fortieth year, I decided to resign my post. My destiny name was Harbhajan Singh—it means "the divine song of God." I had not given enough time to that, to my destiny. Everyone objected. I heard, "You are a fool," "You may not be successful," and "It is impossible." Time has proven them all wrong. My attitude then was, "I don't care if I am successful, or not,, or whether it is impossible. The only possible I know is to be real and be my destiny. I will live somehow, but I will live as I am."

The problem with walking on the spiritual path is that you are tested at every step. Each step expands you, lifts you, and gives you elevation. But on the neurotic path, the path of ego, you enjoy every step, but every step is just flat. No lift, no elevation. You get so tied into it that soon nothing can reach you. Ego is the very capacity to be finite. You say, "I am. These are my things. This is my life. Nobody can tell me anything. I'll do whatever I want to do." In the end it confines you tremendously and tragically. You give no attention to your destiny and lose perspective. You live life through the mind's reactions; you do not feel you as you. You do not penetrate to the soul and live from your heart. You avoid the tests and never gain your uniqueness in your destiny. The immediate pleasures of the ego cut you out of the picture and drag you away from the soul. Choose that path and you will never penetrate through your own mind and see the light of the soul, which is the part of God that is in you.

I understand your insecurities, your desire to not be tested, and your desire for happiness. Your mind becomes satisfied and happy when you get feelings of security on this earth. You think, "My job is good. My car is great. My home is fine. My sex life is good. My blood pressure is fine. My food is good." Everything you have is fine and good. But are you fine? That is harder to answer, but everything hangs on it. You are that you which is above everything. You can never be this, or that. You are that you which is you and you alone. That is the secret of your soul. You must be alert because the mind's reactions can lull you away from that close reality of your soul. That is called temptation. It comes in every form, some subtle, some not.

Often you do not believe yourself and do not trust your destiny. When my book, *The Teachings of Yogi Bhajan*, was written, the person who was to promote it and finish the publication approached me. He said, "We need someone to write the preface. Some actress or important American. Then the book will sell more." I said, "I am the only person to write that preface. These are my teachings, and I am an important American." Now that was a test. I was not speaking from ego. I refused to get into this buy and sell game. I do not need a gimmick. It is a truth, and that truth will sell on its own time by the Guru's Grace. The temptations to succeed, to impress, to control, and to belong are everywhere. If your mind reacts and you have no nail for it, it can make you leave "you as you" behind. When your mind is controlled, every opportunity will come to you as you, in your destiny, and in your spirit.

We claim and hope for a lot of things. When it comes to the test, it is very difficult. We claim we commit to marriage and a graceful relationship. When a problem comes, we run away and become rude and difficult. Each neurotic drama becomes a choice between temptation and consciousness. Which should win? Consciousness and your spirit! But often you know this, and you still let the temptation win and you lose your self. How can you fail your own conscious being? How is this betrayal of your own consciousness possible? It is the same answer: There is a joy in ego because it is now. But the ego is also blind, and that is why there is pain in life.

So what other power can we use to put the hole in the mind? What pearl can focus us beyond the immediacy of the ego? The problem is you cannot control your own mind with your ego. It only produces more of the same and more complications. The Guru tells us this and gives us a tool to control and understand the mind:

ਗੁਰ ਸ਼ਬਦੀ ਇਹ ਮਨ ਹੋੜੀਏ
Gur shabadee eh man horee-ay
  -from a verse of a poet of Guru Gobind Singh's court
This mind can be controlled only with the Guru's Word
—with the Guru's Shabd

It is not just any words. It is special. What is the Guru's *Shabd*? Guru's *Shabd* is words and rhythm and meaning that give you an automatic stamina whenever you face a test, a situation, or a temptation to betray your consciousness. When you train the mind with the Guru's *Shabd*, you develop a condition a faculty called *naam chit aveh*—the identity of your spirit, and God comes to you instantly in your mind. Those words come to you when you are in difficulty, you are in pain, you are in trouble, or you are in a good situation. They come in your mind automatically, like a sprinkle of water. Then it blossoms in you. It establishes an attitude of gratitude. And that gives you a balance and an antidote to the egomaniac mind.

Suppose you do something very good. You think to your self, "God I am great. I am everything." You should feel good. But what should also come to your mind so it doesn't react and become neurotic with the good feelings? The Guru's *Shabd*. Just this one line:

ਤੇਰਾ ਕੀਤਾ ਹੋਏ
Teraa keetaa ho-ay
  -Guru Arjan, *Siri Guru Granth Sahib*, page 522
What you do, that is what happens.

Nothing happens without that great Doer—*Karta Purkh*. Now you can do, feel good, and let it go in its own orbit of effects. Without such a tool the Guru warns us:

ਸੇਵਕ ਸੇਵ ਰਹੇ ਸਚਿ ਰਾਤੇ ਜੋ ਤੇਰੈ ਮਨਿ ਭਾਨੇ
ਦੁਬਿਦਾ ਮਹਲੁ ਨ ਪਾਵੈ ਜਗਿ ਝੂਠੀ ਗੁਣ ਅਵਗਣ ਨ ਪਛਾਨੇ
ਆਪੇ ਮੇਲਿ ਲਏ ਅਕਥੁ ਕਥੀਐ ਸਚੁ ਸਬਦੁ ਸਚੁ ਬਾਣੀ
ਨਾਨਕ ਸਾਚੇ ਸਚਿ ਸਮਾਨੇ ਹਰਿ ਕਾ ਨਾਮੁ ਵਖਾਣੀ

Sayvak sayv rahay sach raatay jo tayrai man bhaanay
Dubedaa mehel na paavai jag jhootee gun avgun na pacchaanay
Aapay mayl la-ay akath kathee-ai sach shabad sach baanee
Naanak saachay sach samaanay har kaa naam vakhaanee

-Guru Amar Das, *Siri Guru Granth Sahib*, page 1233

Your humble servants serve You, O Lord; those who are imbued with the
Truth are pleasing to Your Mind. Those who are involved in duality do not
find a place, they do not find the Mansion of the Lord's Presence.
Wandering and caught in the false nature of the world, they do not
discriminate between merits and demerits.
When the Lord merges us into Himself, we speak the Unspoken Speech.
True is the Shabd, and True is the Word of His Bani.
O Nanak, the true people are absorbed in the Truth;
they utter the Name of the Lord.

Why does this instruction end with such a blessing? What is the wisdom and greatness that comes to those who do the hard work of repeating and meditating on the *naam*? They have gone beyond the reactions of the mind, found the touch of the Infinite in the Guru's *Shabd* and service. This gives them knowledge of the self and being, of soul and Infinity.

With this remembrance and meditation the mind chooses the spirit, chooses grace, and chooses the remote soul as if it is more tangible than anything else. To close this gap of the mind and save your life from the sense of remoteness is the purpose of life! Throughout all your activities, you have to relate, connect, and keep your soul with God. When you are eating, living, waiting, driving, anytime—remember. Let the word guide your mind to synchronize with the Infinite under every mood. With this attitude established you can embrace life and feel the ecstasy of the creation with clarity, humility, and happiness.

The purpose of life is to save your life from the remoteness. You have to keep your soul with God. You have to relate. That is the purpose of life. So when you are eating, when you are living, when you are waiting, when you are driving, you must remember.

The mind loves to feel its power and have you pay attention to it rather than to you and your soul. Suppose you see somebody walking as you are being driven somewhere; or suppose you have an excellent morning meditation practice and someone else does not, then feel God is a little more merciful to you. Be thankful you have the power to be maintained. Then let this *shabd* come to mind to slay pride and let in the power of your innocence and originality:

ਸਮਰਥ ਗੁਰੂ ਸਿਰਿ ਹਥੁ ਧਰਿਓ
ਗੁਰਿ ਕੀਨੀ ਕ੍ਰਿਪਾ ਹਰਿਨਾਮ ਦੀਅਓ ॥ ਜਿਸ ਦੇਖਿ ਚਰੰਨ ਅਘੰਨ ਹਰਿਓ
ਨਿਸਿ ਬਾਸੁਰ ਏਕ ਸਮਾਨ ਧਿਆਨ ॥ ਸੁ ਨਾਮ ਸੁਨੇ ਸੁਤੁ ਭਾਨ ਡਰਿਓ
ਭਨਿ ਦਾਸ ਸੁ ਆਸ ਜਗਤ੍ਰ ਗੁਰੂ ਕੀ ॥ ਪਾਰਸੁ ਭੇਟਿ ਪਰਸੁ ਕਰਿਓ
ਰਾਮਦਾਸੁ ਗੁਰੂ ਹਰਿ ਸਤਿ ਕੀਯਓ ॥ ਸਮਰਥ ਗੁਰੂ ਸਿਰਿ ਹਥੁ ਧਰਿਓ

Samarat guroo sir hat dhari-o
Gur keenee kirpaa harnaam dee-ao. Jis daykh charan agan hari-ao
Nis baasur ayk samaan dhiaan. So naam sunay sut bhaan dari-o
Bhan daas so aas jagatar guroo kee. Paaras bhayt paras kari-o
Raamdas guroo har sat keeyo. Samarat guroo sir hat dhari-o
         - Siri Guru Granth Sahib, page 1400 (*Swaiya* in praise of Guru Ram Das)
The All-Powerful Guru has placed His Hand upon my head.
The Guru has bestowed His Mercy, and blessed me with the Lord's Name.
Seeing His Lotus Feet, my sins are washed away.
Night and day He meditates on the One Lord Alone.
Hearing His Name, Yama (Death), the son of the sun, is afraid.
Says His Slave: Hope lies in the Guru of the World, Guru Amar Das.
He united Ram Das with the philosopher's stone,
and so made him to become the philospher's stone.
By God's Grace, Ram Das is acclaimed as the True Guru.
The All-Powerful Guru placed His Hand upon his head.

The gist of this *shabd* is that the mere touch of the wisdom and blessing of the Guru protects me and gives me the power and opportunity to train my mind to remember *Har*—God's Names. When the Infinite penetrates the mind, it dyes you in the same way. You become vast and see the light of the soul everywhere. Then it is truly true, if you don't see God in all, you don't see God at all.

By the blessing of the Guru's Shabd, may you always uphold your consciousness and walk the path of spirit with every step. May the Guru bless us to serve all those whom we are destined to serve. Give us the scope to reach every heart, every being, and to bring joy and happiness. Thank you for this day and for this evening and this chance to talk and share together. You are the kindest of all kindness. You are Lord of all Lords. May Thy Light guide us each step and all through life.

Sat Naam.

---

[1] The enchantment of the mind is strong when the Positive Mind combines with *ahangkar*. This is the second Aspect of the mind—the Artist. It is as fascinated by painful things as by pleasurable. The mind also projects by chakra. The chakra determines the perceived value from the action. It can be security, intense feelings, control, sympathy, compassion, creativity, identity, devotion, etc. So the effort level is the same, with ups and downs in either case. The difference starts from the structures and biases in the Aspects, Projections, and Facets of the mind.

10 Recognize Your Reality

Sadhana. That is where you sit, dwell in the thoughts and words of the soul, and peel away all your non-reality with the vastness of your spirit. If you train your mind this way, then you will discover something for your self. If you live in absolute fearlessness, God will live in you because fear and truth cannot go together.

Have you ever wondered why your mind reacts so strongly to any effort you make to be still, to become focused on what is important to you, and to let go of minor irritations and emotional upsets? Look no further than this talk to understand your mind's reactions and what to do about them.

10

SADHANA CAN BRING YOUR MIND TO RECOGNIZE YOU AND YOUR reality. It is a crucial question to ask your self: "Is there any non-reality in me?" The answer is, "No!" We are as real as God is. It is our basic nature and conception. So what has happened to us? You are afraid. It starts with your mind. Your mind is afraid that it will be controlled. It creates fear and non-realities to escape you.

That is why it seems so difficult to do a *sadhana*. Rise in the morning, clean your self, exercise, and direct your mind to Infinity. Simple. But the mind knows. It is definitely aware of your effort and even the intentions of the effort. The mind is above time and space. It calculates the impact and consequence. That little act of *sadhana* will contain your mind and make your consciousness the ruler. Your mind through its own nature forms a self-concept of you within the mind. It is an identical identity which is not the real you. *Sadhana* puts you with you. The soul which is Infinite is also above time and space. Your mind knows it. It reacts against that touch of consciousness because it will lose the control, the leverage of the fears.

As soon as you do a *sadhana* you will automatically begin to live more righteously and sensitively. The first sign of that practice is that your "friends" will begin to leave you. Why? Because who are your friends? Normally, your friends are there by fate and circumstance, not by consciousness and commitment. They are friends of your habits. When you become a friend of your consciousness and dwell with God, you do not need friends. You may have many friends. But how could you be lonely? How could you feel needy and form connections out of emotions and temperamental reflexes? That is the truth. Can you confront that truth? Can you realize and live the truth? Yes! Because it is all in you, and *sadhana* can bring your mind to your refinement and reality.

Every human being is by nature very honest. All that dishonesty you see displayed is done out of fear. In your core reality and nature, there is no such thing as dishonesty. There is no such thing as lying. There are many things that have no fundamental existence or necessity. Now this is how it works. When you mix anything in your life with fear, it becomes a non-reality. That is because fear itself is a non-reality. There is nothing foreign, nothing you are not part of, and nothing that is not for you to face. You always want to know what is true. It is your instinct. Truth is that which has no fear. Even a truth spoken in fear is a lie. When you mix fear with anything it becomes non-reality. Your mind links with the ego and instantly creates complex fantasy and side paths. That is why in many spiritual disciplines you have a look, a *bana*, that projects your consciousness, and you are afraid to wear it. You are afraid you will be controlled and that people will ask you for things, seek you out, and demand your top performance and consciousness.

This is a basic personality conflict within you. That conflict is based in fear which is based in non-reality. When you have this conflict, you do not live a human life. You live like a bunch of Mr. Fears and Ms. Fears. All your actions and friendships form out of fear, fear, and more fear. You are not creating from your truth, out of relaxation, and out of love.

Please understand what I am saying. When you become honest within your self and to your self, before your own consciousness, there shall not and cannot be any fear. Once I offered to take a lie detector test. It was the most sophisticated machine run by an expert. He took eight or ten tests by asking me questions and watching the output from the recording pens. Every question showed that I lied. No matter what he asked. He asked, "How can this be? Many questions are absolutely true and simple facts. We both know that."

I said, "Go ahead. Ask more questions if you want. You will not find a single positive test. You told me this machine is perfect and can tell you if I am telling the truth or not. I just showed you that this machine says I am lying all the time regardless of what I say."

He said, "How is that possible? It is completely objective."

I said, "I have added a little fear to every statement. That lie detector doesn't test whether you lie or tell the truth. It tests your fear. And if you happen to be a very sensitive person, then even the remotest fear that you are being subjected to the test will record the fear as a lie. It must come through the machine. The poor machine has no choice and no consciousness to know the difference. It is more blind than justice."

You all have that much blindness when you do not use your consciousness to confront your mind with your reality. Once a great painter came to a swami to show his new painting. He was very prideful and insecure about it. He wasn't certain if it was great and how people would like it. He went to the swami for a neutral opinion. The painter pulled out the painting and said, "Look, Swami-ji, at what I have accomplished."

The swami said, "Where should I look."

He said, "There." But he pointed to the wrong side of the room.

The swami said, "I don't see any painting there. The painting is on the opposite side."

The painter said, "I can't see it myself. I have suddenly gone blind."

The swami said, "You wanted me to see it, and you can't see it yourself. Be blessed. Unless you stop this fear you'll never see the reality you created."

He was temporarily blind. His own pride filled him with fear and anxiety. His ego locked his mind and created a huge pressure so the optic nerve stopped functioning. That happens to us all the time. We go temporarily blind and temporarily deaf. We become temporarily unintelligent. We cut ourselves off from our reality and our creativity and live in the non-reality of a dream world created with our fears. That is the whole problem. God never made you to suffer and never gave you the mind to create such tortures.

Religions were supposed to give you a technology to regain your reality and tame the mind. You have been betrayed many times by false teachers and by inadequate technology for the mind. One of the greatest acts ever done on the religious level to give you wisdom and reality was by Guru Gobind Singh, the tenth teacher of the Sikh way. He gave you directly to the Word, to the *Naad* of the *Siri Guru Granth Sahib*. He confirmed the technology to take you beyond fear and beyond the personality conflict within you. And he gave you no personality to be afraid of in a person. When you read and listen to the words in the *Siri Guru Granth Sahib*, it is nothing but your own infinite personality. Your mind dwells in your consciousness. When you read and recite it you always hear the truth, and hear it regardless of the state and strategies of your mind. It is beyond time and space. When you begin and you read the words, *Ek ong kaar*, there is one Infinite consciousness in all creation, it is your presence. The *Siri Guru Granth Sahib* is your Infinite presence. In the presence of the *Siri Guru Granth Sahib*, you read like this:

ੴ ਸਤਿਗੁਰ ਪ੍ਰਸਾਦਿ
ੴ ਸਤਿਨਾਮੁ ਕਰਤਾ ਪੁਰਖੁ ਨਿਰਭਉ ਨਿਰਵੈਰੁ
ਅਕਾਲ ਮੂਰਤਿ ਅਜੂਨੀ ਸੈਭੰ ਗੁਰਪ੍ਰਸਾਦਿ ॥ ਜਪੁ
ਆਦਿ ਸਚੁ ਜੁਗਾਦਿ ਸਚੁ ॥ ਹੈ ਭੀ ਸਚੁ ਨਾਨਕ ਹੋਸੀ ਭੀ ਸਚੁ
ਸੋਚੈ ਸੋਚਿ ਨ ਹੋਵਈ ਜੇ ਸੋਚੀ ਲਖ ਵਾਰ....

Ek ong kaar sat gur prasaad
Ek ong kaar sat naam, kartaa purakh, nirbhao, nirvair,
akaal moorat, ajoonee, saibhang, gur prasaad. Jap!
Aad sach, jugaad sach, hai bhee sach, naanak hosee bhee sach
Sochai soch na hovee jai sochee lakh vaar....

-Guru Nanak, the first words of *Siri Guru Granth Sahib*, page 1

There is one Creator and this is the gift of that One True Guru.
The Creator of all is One, Truth is His Name, He is the Doer of everything,
fearless and revengeless, undying, unborn, and self-illumined.
This is revealed through the True Guru's Grace. Meditate!
True in the beginning, True through all the ages, True even now,
O Nanak, He shall ever be True.
By thinking and thinking upon the nature of God,
no knowledge of Him is ever attained....

You can sit and read from the *Siri Guru Granth Sahib* yourself. There is no conflict with any other person. There is no personality to confront. Then the reality of you within you is in reach. It is that core personality of you, your consciousness that you must recognize. Then the mind will not amplify and manipulate your fears. The moment you have no fear, when you are fearless and revengeless, you are the living God. God does not live off in some heavens. God lives in every heart. In hearts where there is fear, then God is in trouble, and non-reality brings a lot of pain.

What happens between God and you? What happens when this soul of yours comes to this planet? When you, the light of the soul, come in the soul to experience this creation what occurs? There are five layers of ether. The first, most dense and tangible layer of the ether is when the soul cleans itsself and has a receptivity to prepare itself to go back according to its karmas and projections. The soul is held by the subtle body so it is neither in earth nor gone into merger in the One.

In the second layer of ether, the soul is content to stay, supervise, and help other promising souls. It acts beyond space, beyond its own personal domain.

In the third layer of ether, a soul vibrates in the pure light of the soul to reach liberation and to uplift all souls now, past, and future. It goes through and beyond time. It is these three ethers that a meditative mind can easily penetrate. Doing the many meditations that refine the mind gives you the capacity to experience this. It is not mystical, it is practical.

Between the third and the fourth layers of ether it is a bit tricky. You can slip into the fourth layer and not be able to come back. You are drawn into a merger and lose the separateness of normal experience. That is why in the ambrosial hours of the morning when people of God leave their body to bless all, their physical bodies are always guarded. At that time any imbalance can create a disturbance and they may not return.

The fourth layer of ether is the Light of God itself. The stretch of the atoms to existence. The fifth layer is nothing but God, Being itself.

When the soul leaves this fifth ether and travels into an incarnation, it comes to this planet not to seek anything. It comes to recognize the God, recognize its consciousness, and experience the creation. All the reactions and commotions and attempts to control are not required. All the fears that you have something to gain and to lose are misplaced. That is why as the soul was to leave the total merger, God gave it the mind and certain lessons.

The story of the soul's journey is recounted like this. As the soul was told to go it hesitated. It asked God, "What if I need you immediately and there is no time at all? What can I do?" It was then that God gave the first lesson of the soul. God said, "Just recognize me. Say to your self, 'I am the God'." There is no real separation between you and God. You are only now seeking to understand and experience your self as part of God with a sole proprietorship on the soul. Instead you still want to be recognized for your hairdo, your car, your this, and that. You act like you are blind and emotional jerks. Then the soul asked, "I am part of You and you are part of me. But what if all that time and space get in between us? What can I do?" God said, "Don't worry. I have given you the mind. It is faster than time and space. You can reach me no matter where you are. The mind will serve you three ways. When it is neutral it will recognize the truth. When it is positive it will tell you the right direction to go and what good can be done. When it is negative it will warn you and protect you from harm and badness."

The mind is your servant to master time and space and to always find a way to connect with the Infinite. To tap this intelligence in the mind say to your self: "I am Thee. Thou is Me. Me is Thou. I am Thee." Play with it. Repeat it in rhythm. It has the *naad*. It penetrates the subconscious and reminds you that you are neither alone nor separated. Then the soul wondered, "What if I have forgotten all this? How can I remember?" Close your eyes and speak truthfully, and for God's sake feel it. Speak it fearlessly and with your whole heart. When you are caught in time and space say, "God and Me, Me and God are One." Every layman can say it. Put your mind and emotion in it.

You are never separated from God or your soul. You come to this planet not to seek anything. You come to recognize God and realize your soul. That is where your training and the religions have failed you. You were brainwashed to believe you had to seek God or seek Truth, as if you were not part of that and did not already have it. I know this may seem against every tradition: Christianity, Islam, Hinduism, Judaism, and even Buddhism. But that is only how you have learned.

The person who came as a God man or God's man and directly spoke out against this lie was Guru Nanak, the first teacher of the Sikh way. He said:

ਆਦਿ ਸਚੁ ਜੁਗਾਦਿ ਸਚੁ ॥ ਹੈ ਭੀ ਸਚੁ ਨਾਨਕ ਹੋਸੀ ਭੀ ਸਚੁ
Aad sach, jugaad sach, hai bhee sach, nanak hosee bhee sach
  -Guru Nanak, *Siri Guru Granth Sahib*, page 1, from *Mul Mantra*
True in the beginning, True through all the ages, True even now,
O Nanak, He shall ever be True.

He was one person filled with God's divine light whose mind was perfectly clear, and he could say the truth. That is a function of a Guru—to dispel the darkness. And what is your darkness? Fear. When you act out of fear you try to draw attention to yourself out of any insanity you can create. Seeking the attention comes from your darkness and insanity. Creativity and love come from your sensitivity. A developed sensitivity in character gives you commitment. Commitment in turn gives you more sensitivity of character. They are interrelated. That is how this planet runs. No matter how many millions of suns rise and moons come, there will still be darkness without the touch of the Guru.

I know this can be hard to hear. Some people are afraid to speak with me or any truthful person. But I am not against anybody. People are afraid, because when you hear truth, you also get exposed to your own lies. You don't want to hear that. All right, it is a choice. Don't hear it now. One day time will tell you in another way. That will be very painful. I serve the House of the Guru. I will still be here, sitting and serving. Why won't you be as God made you to be? Why won't you just go and be who you are? Why not recognize your reality rather than pretend and project differently than you are?

Which brings us back to *sadhana*. That is where you sit, dwell in the thoughts and words of the soul, and peel away all your non-reality with the vastness of your spirit. If you train your mind this way, then you will discover something for your self. If you live in absolute fearlessness, God will live in you because fear and truth cannot go together.

Sat Naam.

11 Live Consciously Conscious

Everything else you have been told so far is totally W-R-O-N-G! You are not a body, not a mind, not a soul, not God, and definitely not a devil. Every normal person thinks, imagines, and projects through his mind. He ultimately identifies with the mind and becomes dependent on the mind. The reality is that he should not depend on his mind. Instead, he should project from the point of view of his consciousness. When you live consciously conscious with mind and consciousness balanced, you develop a capacity for sensitivity we call reverence. Then relationships are healing, wise, and productive.

The unique line these talks take is between the practical details of the technology of meditation and Kundalini Yoga and the grand concepts of the philosophy of mind and spirit. This talk focuses on the practical task of living these concepts, of challenging the automatic mechanisms of the mind, of creating a life worth living with joy and gratitude. The impact of all these talks is to get us to be a little more angelic and a little less animal each day, in each act and in each of our words. The beauty of this series is how practical the tools of meditation are and how clearly the abstract realities of the mind are embodied in everyday discourses.

11

YOU ARE NOTHING BUT A POTENTIAL LIVING CONSCIOUSNESS. Your basic necessity, the drive of your elemental self is to become a practical, grassroots, living consciousness—potential living consciousness to practical living consciousness. Everything else you have been told so far is totally W-R-O-N-G! You are not a body, not a mind, not a soul, not God, and definitely not a devil. Every normal person thinks, imagines, and projects through the mind. You ultimately identify with your mind and become dependent on the mind. The reality is that you should not depend on your mind. Instead, you should project from the point of view of your consciousness. You have been so trained and brainwashed that you can't relate to yourself as a living consciousness. You do not even have the concept. If you do not depend directly on your consciousness, you are not you at all. When you are not you in the beginning and core of each action, then there is nothing you can do which will be true, and there is nothing you can do which can make you happy.

Perhaps you do not understand one fundamental fact: you, as a living consciousness, are subject to time and space. It takes time to do something and it requires space to do it in. But the mind by nature is faster than time and space. This is a split. You depend on the mind, but you cannot rely on it. It takes a thought and magnifies it, twists it left and right, and creates many short cuts, illusions, dreams, and temptations. It creates a mirage, and asks you to walk on it! It will put you deep into that pit, and then you don't have a chance. The mind is too fast.

That is the problem with you. You always want to take the chance. Then you suffer and get desperate and take another chance and suffer even more. It is endless, seductive, and tragic. If you do not find that ground where you and your mind can meet, you become nothing but a suffering man. Now, I have nothing against a suffering man. He is okay. He is worth your friendship and you should take him to dinner. The problem will be that in the center of all that suffering is emptiness, a big heap of mental poop. Worse yet it is half-digested poop!

Think of a time when you rushed through lunch. Your mind was already done with the lunch and on to business. But your mouth had not finished chewing, breaking the food into small bits, bathing those bits in digestive fluids, and preparing the rest of your system to receive them. The result was a stomach-ache, half-digested food, and bad smells. You and your mind must meet. If you rush ahead of your time and space, if you depend on the shortcuts your mind projects, your life will be half digested, and you will carry a bad smell.

You will not deliver your destiny—the inner urge to be and be you. Then you won't make any sense to your self or to anyone else. I knew someone, David, who was very rich—millions and millions. Someone asked me, "Where is David So-and-So?" I said, "Oh, that millionaire. He died over two years ago." No one really missed him. All people remember is that he made millions of dollars. Then he died. That is it. His son sold his carefully designed house for dollars. Everything is liquidated and distributed. His car is gone, his house is gone, his property is gone, and his collections are gone. Even his wife is remarried, and his children are gone, but they never visited him while he was alive anyway. He generated a lot of things. His mind magnified his attachments and skills. In the end what will be the impact, the reality, and the legacy? You produce a life full of things, but you are absent. It is a life with no juice, no essence, no heart, and no reality. It lacks confidence, penetration, and impact. The mind was given to you to relate to Infinity, and consciousness was given to you to live. If you react and project mentally, and then depend on that, you as you are just zero. Anything multiplied by zero will become zero. With this habit even your elemental personality will eventually become zero and leave no trace.

Your mind acts through three Functional Minds, each with its own form and characteristics: Negative, Positive, and Neutral. With these Functional Minds, your mind will push and pull you anyway it wants. Your mind can trick you and create mazes that you can't believe. It can take away all your physical, personal, and spiritual pride. It can drag you like a dead rat, and you will not know it. It can make you feel belittled. The mind, in one second, can swing you from the North Pole to the South Pole. It can make you see things that are totally irrelevant or insignificant as the only important facts in your life. The mind is more powerful than your estimate, more than you can think, imagine, or even feel. This blind spot happens because whatever your ego feels, the mind interprets it, expands it, and shrinks it. The mind, faster than fast, automatically interprets each feeling according to its own frequency and according to the chakra it is relating to.

You are human beings. Why do you have to act like desperate idiots? Why? It is not a requirement. It is not a necessity. The nub of the problem is you do not have the habit to relate to consciousness consciously. You need to build in a habit for conscious living. This is a great and practical truth, a basic principle in Humanology: when you relate to consciousness your neuroses will fall away. No one who starts to relate to consciousness can be neurotic at all. What is it like to live as a neurotic? Neurotic people are angry people. Neurotic people are deceitful. They lie. They act unfriendly, and they are often merciless. When you interlock with your mind and become neurotic, it is a complicated affair. There are 36 other qualities that invalidate and disqualify you as a conscious being. Your anger and ego get stuck together. That is the usual way you become neurotic. You can change this. When you bring your soul and your will together you become conscious. It is all you and it is all about you. When you live consciously, you make a choice. That choice has to be valid and fully from the heart; a choice without duality and with complete clarity. Then you direct your mind—your head—to act on it. You direct your mind to commit and go for the goal you choose.

This is a way of living. It is a relationship to your mind from your consciousness. You should try to practice with a simple homework assignment. Sit down and on a sheet of paper create four columns. In the first column write down any subject or question of your life. Then in the three remaining columns write down your comments, feelings, and thoughts from three perspectives. Be direct and honest in each mental position. Write your Personal Choice, then write from your Sentimental and Emotional Choice, and lastly write from your Conscious Choice. If you write cut and dried, straight, and honestly, you may be surprised to find how different you are on each issue.

I say to you today, if God has blessed you with a desire for conscious living and has given you a spiritual path, then take it. Walk with it. Excel in it. Grow with it. Then the most fascinating experience is that everything will grow with you.

At any stage of our life, if we can very sincerely and very honestly relate to the integrity of our own consciousness and start living consciously, we will start living happily. When we connect to that integrity, we will project that consciousness along well-defined paths and conceptions of our self. The one who works and makes others to work selflessly is a Karma Yogi. One who lives religiously and inspires others to join is a *Dharam* Yogi. One who dwells in God each moment of life and makes others to dwell in God is a *Brahm* Yogi. One who understands the subtlety and the great essence of life is a *rishi*. One who has mastered his *tattvas* and the use of all nine gates is a swami. One who lives in truth, practices truth, and spreads truth is a Sikh. One whose personality is filled with radiance and who projects truth by his or her presence is a Khalsa. These paths and conceptions are well-defined, well created, and well-documented. They establish conscious living, giving you a chance. You all have a chance with this body, mind, and breath. It is a priceless chance, not a million- or billion-dollar chance, but a chance worth trillions of dollars.

What is it like to live with this habit to relate from your consciousness? Hate nobody; love everybody. It won't cost you anything. Love never costs anything. Love is the most selfish act. It gives you so much protection, grace, and radiance. It doesn't give you any smallness or suffering. The attitude of conscious living is to love and give grace to someone worthy of your trust. Even if you know a person who is hopeless and good for nothing, still love him. Never trust him. You have that right; that is up to your own conscience and intuition.

When you come from your consciousness, you need not match those who do not, and who are caught in the tangle of reactions to their own emotions. You will meet some people who will tell you, "I am leaving you. I don't care. You are nobody." But those who belittle you and try to bring you down are just dogs of the time. They have to bark. They are emotional creeps who can not do anything but what they do. Love them any way. Be confident of your own consciousness and let life be vast and creative as it is.

This may seem hard but your dog cannot cook food for you, can he? Still you love him. You have to feed him dog food, right? He cannot dance with you. He cannot go to parties. Your dog can not do millions of things. You find a way to love him anyway. What happens if another human does the same thing? They bark; they have teeth; they cannot do anything; and they do not understand your consciousness. Don't get hurt by trusting them. Do offer trust to life. When you cannot trust, then at least love. Hatred will go against you and kill you. Vengeance will ruin and cripple you. Anger will rend and cripple your body, and initiate every disease. Your mind may drop those angers and mistrusts, but they leave a scar in the body and wear it down, so live with lightness and patience.

When you live consciously conscious with mind and consciousness balanced, you develop a sensitivity we call reverence. Then relationships are healing, wise, and productive. But in this country I have seen that almost every relationship is emotional and temperamental. There is a tremendous lack of reverence. Once I surveyed a dozen or so people. I asked, "How can you knowingly and rudely abuse somebody, and then expect that one minute later that same person will talk to you and make any sense." The answer was, "In this country that is our normal way of speaking. Abuse and familiarity are our norms in communication." Can you believe that? I couldn't believe it. It is communication without consciousness or relationship to the consciousness and subtlety that is you. If somebody takes advantage of the privilege to communicate, and just abuses, lays his number, or dumps his subconscious, that person has fallen from grace—his own grace! I learned this from a teacher.

Once I was in a class with my teacher. He was in the middle of a lecture. A student knocked at the door and interrupted the lesson. My teacher banished that student from seeing him for one year. We felt it was too harsh to banish him for one year. We understood that he was called, and that he had come to learn. Our teacher said, "This is also learning. Whenever you go for wisdom and truth, be very humble. Empty yourself. Go to a saintly or a wise person humbly so that you can fulfill yourself." You see, we had a special understanding. On Thursdays our teacher allowed us *guruwar*, an open house, where we could talk any non-sense or question that we wanted, but it would be spoken and discussed within the framework of reverence and alertness. The great lesson for that student was that he didn't have the courtesy to wait for the guard and ask him if he could disturb the lecture or not. He lacked the attitude of reverence and that limited him to learn, then and there—on the spot. That was the kindness of that teacher to catch him before time and life would catch him later. We lack that training in our communication. We lack that pattern to use our speech, to alert our mind, to relate to our consciousness, grace, and awareness.

If you live with that attitude of reverence for your self and all others, you will be healthier, happier, and more effective. Live consciously. Try it as an experiment for one week. Test it. Relate to others from your consciousness and nothing else. You will be surprised how great a load you will drop. In just one week without emotional and commotional interlocking, with your mind alert and conscious, experience how light you will feel. As that load drops, you will feel totally new, and even sickness will drop away before your eyes.

Take a chance and live consciously. Be light and polite and beautiful, just as Guru Amar Das showed us by serving all. Call all your friends and three people that you hate the most, and be kind and clear. Share your self and the feeling to just act and speak with reverence and love. It is called conscious living, and it gives you and your mind vastness in reality.

Sat Naam.

12 Master the 81 Facets

12

The Nature of the Mind

Success, happiness, and constant prosperity are the result of mastering the mind. The mind exists as a servant to your soul. When the mind is aligned with the soul, each thought that is stimulated from the intellect to eventually manifest into life is perceived and acted on with clarity and reality. You will be happy and fulfilled in your life. But the mind is also a vast mechanism with its own characteristics and its own momentum. When the mind is full of unconscious identifications, emotions, projections, intentions, and attachments, the thought is perceived for other than what it is. This masked thought becomes the basis of many false judgements and fruitless commitments that lead to unhappiness and frustrations in life.

Most of us have not looked at our own mind. We haven't taken it on to study and to master. The reason is simple. We are very busy using the mind. It is like the eye. We see with it all the time and do not bother to examine it until we have a problem. Even then we leave it to the doctor and do not become opthamalogists. But the mind is different. It is a universal process and capacity that we use most personally. We each have a special access to that mind and its contents that others do not. Since we look at the world and even at the mind using the mind, it acts like a filter for all of our experience. If it is distorted or fractured in any way, it affects everything we do and it constrains what we can do.

Unlike observations about the body, our observations about the mind lack a clear consensus. With the body we can watch its movements and pick out its organs and key features easily. When we turn our attention to the mind it is another story. There are many theories and many maps of the parts of the mind. There are many ways to study the mind. It can be approached as a study of the brain with EEG, PET, MRI, and SPECT technologies to get images of the activity of brain areas, pathways, and even individual cells. It can be approached as something beyond the brain to be encountered through states of consciousness, feelings, imagery, dreams, and stories. And it can be approached as something else entirely, through deep meditation and the use of intuition. The approach you take depends on your final use for what you will find.

Regardless of your approach and your theory, one thing we all share is the encounter with the experience of our own mind when we begin our day. We experience our mind as we make choices under every condition of emotion and challenge. We need practical know-how that lets us direct and use our mind. That is where the applied psychology and techniques of Humanology are useful for each of us no matter which particular theory of the mind we subscribe to.

When you finally decide to invest a little time to encounter your mind, what do you notice? Just sit still for a minute. Close your eyes. Bring your attention to alert and notice all your thoughts and sensations without reacting to them. The mind is noisy. The yogis say it releases a thousand thoughts in the blink of an eye. There are sensations, emotions, thoughts, sensory impressions, conversations with your self, memories, fantasies, intuitions, psychic impressions, and more.

Here are a few basic characteristics you should know as you prepare to train and conquer your mind. First, it is largely automatic. Since the mind is fast, and beyond the categories of time and space, it supports your actions with many more thoughts than you could ever act on. The result of this is that it is not you who think. Your mind thinks, not you. It floods you with thoughts, both wanted and unwanted, intended and unintended. Not all thoughts support the you which is you. You are awareness itself and not all these thoughts. You are actually carried through the soul.

Second, the mind is ever moving. If it stops it cannot function. It is not a local phenomenon. Just like in the ocean you can feel waves that were generated from a far away distance, so in the mind you have thoughts and feelings from the entire universe and every other person. The places and people you are most attuned to and attached to are what usually fill your stream of thoughts. As you become more neutral and non-attached the scope of those thoughts and feelings widens.

Third, the mind functions best on contrasts. It seeks polarities and tends to classify things in pairs, in positive and negative, in good and bad. Consider your eyes. They constantly move with motions called saccadic motion. If this is stopped artificially with a drug, you cannot see. Your eyes need the movement to provide contrasts and comparisons so your nervous system can construct your vision. It is the same with the mind. It seeks contrast and polarity. Since the mind is impersonal as well as personal, you find this search for contrast and extremes throughout nature.

Fourth and last, the mind is just as material as the body, only it is subtler. Water exists in degrees of subtlety from vapor to liquid to ice. Just so, you can think of the mind as the vapor, the feelings as water, and the neurons and connections as ice. The mind is a structure, a process, and an energy that lets your awareness operate and manifest in this creation. You can observe it and you can change it. You can affect it with gross things like food, powerful things like breath, and subtle things like thought. It has its own flow, structure, and metabolism.

The mind itself does not stop. That is why "a point of stillness" is one of the essential tools you need to look into the mind. This is where special techniques, like meditation, mantra, and breath control are needed. Using the mind to try and convince the mind to be still is like stopping a hurricane by blowing at it. There is too much going on. A further difficulty is that you use your mind to observe your mind. Just imagine two mirrors facing each other at a slight angle. If you put a candle in between and look into the mirror, you can see hundreds of candles, reflections upon reflections. The mind can reflect back on itself and create images within images, thoughts within thoughts.

We need to be able to affect the mind without getting caught in an infinite self-reference. To do that, we need to understand the structure of the mind, recognize the origin of thought, and consciously determine which thoughts are consistent with our true self. We have outlined the art and science to synchronize the 81 Facets of the mind through the use of meditation. Facets of your mind regulate the reactions of the personality, body, and mind to each thought. If the 81 Facets can be controlled so that the mind perceives each thought clearly, then the mind can align with the intention of the soul. The result is effectiveness, inner and outer peace, and awakened intuition.

Concept of the Mind

In classical yoga philosophy, the soul is accompanied on its journey from God through the creation by the mind.

Look at the **Cosmic Law of Manifestation and Being** diagram. *[See next page]*. You can follow the journey of the soul from top to bottom in this diagram. The mind is part of nature, *Prakirti. Prakirti*, which includes both material and mind, is composed of and governed by the three primary qualities called the *gunas*. The three *gunas* are *sattva, rajas,* and *tamas. Sattva* is subtle, sublime, clear, neutral, and pure. *Tamas* is heavy, contaminated, confused, concealed, and slow. *Rajas* is fiery, active, initiating, and has the power of transformation.

Cosmic Law of Manifestation and Being

The origin and seed of all we experience is unmanifest and subtle. First is consciousness, then vibration, then separation into the three forces or Gunas. Then the blending of elements and thoughts manifests in the world of the senses, emotions and matter.

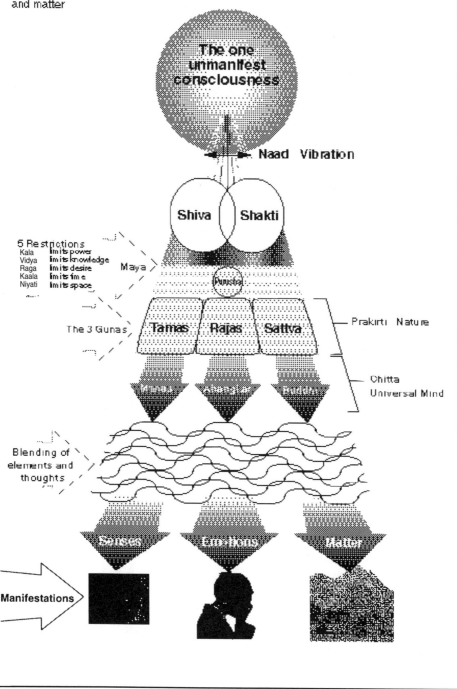

While *rajas* is active, it transforms *sattva* to *tamas* and *tamas* to *sattva*. These three qualities constantly intertwine, intermingle, intermix, contrast, advance, and withdraw in various combinations with each other. It is these special combinations of quality that exist before the manifestation of things or thoughts. They underlie all things in creation.

The three *gunas* operate to create the Universal Mind, *chitta*. Think of this Universal Mind as a vast ocean, full of waves and vortexes, that stores the impact of every action and thought. This vast *chitta* is divided into three major functions that reflect the three *gunas*. The *sattva guna* is reflected in the *buddhi* part of mind. *Buddhi* perceives reality, discerns what is real from unreal, assesses neutrally, and makes judgments from the perspective of your Infinite identity. It represents heavenly phenomena in activity of totality as totality. The *rajasic guna* is reflected in *ahangkar*. *Ahangkar* is the part of the mind that gives identity through attachment and boundaries. It gives the sense of ego, of boundary, of containment, and the beginning of identity to the various blends of the *gunas*. It represents, in its most positive sense, the heavenly activity of the coexistence of "totality within a vacuum," for at this point it is unmanifested. Totality within a vacuum means that there are no boundaries or other defining aspects to contain the totality. Instead, all the qualities are mixed, and are defined by their own combinations among themselves. The third *guna, tamas,* is reflected in the aspect of mind called *manas*. This is the lower mind, the sensory mind. It is the one most commonly dealt with by the psychologists in contemporary times. It stores the images, sounds, feelings, and smells of all the senses and their combinations in reactive and creative sequences. It also includes subconscious reactions, mental entanglements, and commotions. This represents the heavenly activity of the coexistence of totality within the finite.

The next movement of the *gunas* creates the remaining levels to link the soul and mind to the earth realms. The soul passes through gradual stages from the one unmanifested consciousness to gross manifestation. It finally connects to the densest condensations of those stages—the five last *tattvas*: ether, air, fire, water, and earth. It is these gross qualities that we can perceive in the qualities of earthly existence. The *tattvas* give a condition to the mind, and the mind can balance the *tattvas*. It is a back and forth relationship. These five *tattvas* give qualities to the manifestation of mind into our senses, actions, and perceptions.

The mind takes on a particular blend of qualities in association with each thought that passes through it. The blend of qualities is the result of the relative levels of activity of the *gunas* and the *buddhi, ahangkar,* and *manas* capacities of the mind. Individuals, through their experience in the world, and through their reactions to their own mental phenomena, create various impressions that are recorded in the subconscious and the superconscious minds. This accumulation of actions and reactions creates a kind of momentum in the mind. So the mind does not start from zero. It has a perception already focused on specific categories or features of experience, even before a thought is generated. If the thought that is issued from the intellect does not perfectly agree with the long established momentum of the mind, the mind reacts by projecting a particular blend of colors around that thought. That color then interacts with the personality, projection, and interactions of that individual.

Generation of a Thought

Now imagine the soul giving a radiant impulse to the mind to have *manas, ahangkar*, and *buddhi* activate the intellect to produce a thought. When that thought is released through the intellect, which is part of the mind, it produces feelings, which produce emotions, which then result in desires, which lead to action. This sequence of manifestation is universal.

Each thought that is produced in the intellect is like a well-crafted sculpture. It has its own form, its own dimension, and its own internal structure. Each thought has an *antar*, which is the essence. This *antar,* has a characteristic *jantar*, which is dimensional proportion. And it has a specific *bantar. Bantar* means the kind of structure that supports it. Just as when you are building a house, only certain kinds of wood will be suitable for the main beams, and others for shingles. Just so, a thought can only be constructed by the application of specific intensities of the senses and other qualities. Each thought also has a characteristic *mantar* (mantra), or sound vibration, and *yantar*, its visual form or radiance. All of these add together to form a single congruent and powerful projected reality that elaborates the thought. That is its essence. Whenever you can act in reality to the thought at its structural essence, you gain power over those thoughts, and the power to manifest or to block the manifestation of those thoughts.

But there is a problem. You do not see the thought for what it is. You mistake it for something else and do not use the power and structure within its essence. The intellect is always releasing thoughts. At the same time, the soul has a presence that induces the mind to serve it by releasing thoughts aligned with its intention. However, the mind has biases, attachments, and blends of actions and reactions in the subconscious gathered through experience. When the thought is released, the mind cloaks it with the 81 Facets that are a complex blend of *manas, ahangkar,* and *buddhi,* with the Positive, Negative, and

Neutral Minds. All your reactions and habits recorded in the subconscious are added to that thought.

The universal release of thought from the intellect, which then goes to feelings and emotions, then to desire and on to action, has two points at which the will that comes from the soul can be applied. Between emotion and desire, you can be attached or unattached to the specific thought that is going through the sequence. Most meditation is applied at that juncture, because to get emotion to become desire the element of *ahangkar* and personal attachment must be added. The other place that will is effective is exactly at the release point of intellect to thought. This is the same place that the Facets of the mind automatically apply themselves. If will is applied at that level, the mind is trained to surrender the cloud around the thought, and to bring the color around the thought to clear or to white, so that it can be perceived as it is.

The **Cycle of the Intellect** diagram *[see next page]* represents the path of a thought through your mind and then into actions in the world. It represents our normal experience but slowed down so we can see each part of the process. First there is the Universal Mind. We are just in it, like a fish in the ocean. We don't go to the mind; the mind is everywhere we are. In that universal ocean of the mind, there are always waves—thoughts. The "intellect" in the diagram doesn't mean an intellectual analysis of something. It means the mind is always stirred up, turbulent, and it is that turbulence which we experience as thought. As the thought is created and released, it is cloaked. The cloaking also comes from the mind. The cloak is made up of other thoughts and feelings. Those are usually from the greater unconscious of the mind—from habits of the mind that are so automatic we don't consciously think of them. We can become aware of them or not, but they are there, built in right from the beginning.

Depending on how thick the cloaking, we may see the thought that was released from the intellect for what it is or we may confuse it for something else. All this happens in our own mind. We could have a thought and not understand our selves. We could be clouded over with so many of the 81 Facets that we act confused and out of touch with our feelings and purpose. Next, the cloaked thought is processed by other parts of the mind and it associates with many other thoughts, memories, sensations and feelings. This forms a final feeling and emotion.

Then something interesting happens. We decide if this thought and its feelings are ours. Did someone else, the television perhaps, just sneak this thought in or do we stand behind it and own it? We either attach to the thought, or we let it go by like so much background noise. If it goes by, nothing much hap-

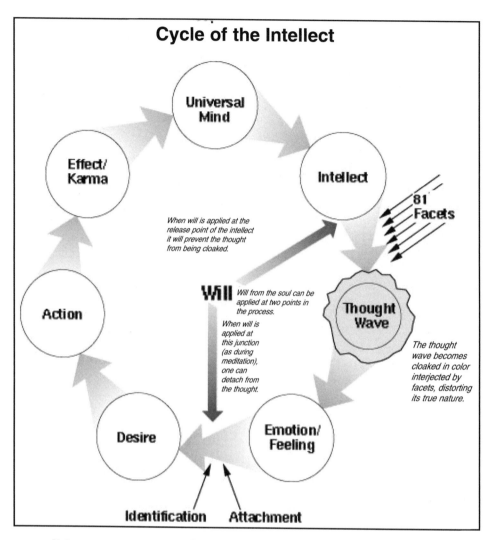

Cycle of the Intellect

Universal Mind

Effect/ Karma

Intellect

81 Facets

When will is applied at the release point of the intellect it will prevent the thought from being cloaked.

WILL *Will from the soul can be applied at two points in the process.*

When will is applied at this junction (as during meditation), one can detach from the thought.

Action

Thought Wave

The thought wave becomes cloaked in color interjected by facets, distorting its true nature.

Desire

Emotion/ Feeling

Identification   Attachment

pens. It is one more wave in the ocean. It may affect the general condition of the mind, but it doesn't create a specific impact. If you decide, either consciously or unconsciously, that this thought is yours, then the feeling changes. It becomes a desire. Your glands get involved. Neural mechanisms start to trigger muscles and make plans. You move into some action. Once the thought is this far along, it is hard to stop. You have all the momentum of glands and muscle behind it now. If you want to alter it, it is better to intercede farther back near the origin or at the point of attachment.

The last bubble in the diagram says, "Effect/Karma." Each action has a reaction we call karma. That impact is recorded as a momentum in your mind. Each action creates more actions like it or like its polarity. There is a whole mechanism. Each thought when acted upon creates a cosmic echo. It has to have a consequence. That is the action of karma. The only other choice at this point in the diagram is if the action you do corresponds to the intentions and purpose of your soul and is in tune with the larger universe when you do it. It is like creating a wave that blends in perfectly to the created flow. Then you have no reaction. It is smooth and without internal noise in the mind. That is called an action of dharma. In either case, what you do is recorded and stored in the Universal Mind, since it is everywhere. This then affects the next thought released and the type of cloaking that goes on. It is a powerful cycle and central to creating a successful and happy life.

Each of the 81 Facets of mind produces a specific cloaking action on the thoughts released by the intellect. That cloaking produces a lack of clarity, a lack of accurate response to the real nature of each thought. It is this split between the actual structure of the thought and the nature of the color that surrounds it, that produces so much pain from people's inappropriate actions. When we are not clear and conscious at the release of a thought, we are not conscious of the impact and consequences of that thought. When the consequences do come, we do not want to accept them. We get depressed and feel alienated from our life.

81 Facets of the Mind

Most people want to change personal feelings, habits, and emotional attitudes. The concept of the mind we outlined so far is helpful, but there is a crucial gap in the map of the mind between the impersonal realms of *Buddhi, Ahangkar,* and *Manas* and the cloaking of an individual thought through our mind. If we can understand how our personal reactions and feelings create the 81 Facets that cloak our thoughts, then we can find ways to identify our personal patterns of emotions and habits. Then we can use appropriate meditations to strengthen, refine, or balance the parts of the mind that underlie the behaviors we want to change. The key to this is how the three Functional Minds, Negative, Positive, and Neutral, interact with each other and with the three Impersonal Minds, *buddhi, ahangkar, and manas.* This interaction generates Aspects, Projections, and Facets. These form the basis of the personal psychology that we all experience. They shape our habits, attitudes, reactivity, skills, and our emotional stance toward the world and toward our selves. Now let's examine the Functional Minds and how they generate the Facets and Projections of the mind, and open a whole new world of how to deal with your mind. This is part of the technology of Kundalini Yoga and the use of the *Shabd Guru* that is priceless, as we face the pressures from our growth as humanity and as individuals in the Aquarian Age.

As the soul journeys through nature, it is contained by a body called the subtle body. It is like a very thin skin that goes with it even after the physical body dies. It also has three bodies that allow it to experience the mind and to preserve its sense of self. They are bodies for the Negative Mind, the Positive Mind, and the Neutral Mind. These three Functional Minds are fundamental modes of reaction by the individual soul's mind. They write your individual signature into the Universal Mind by expressing your reactions to things, thoughts, and feelings.

The Negative Mind is the fastest. It is the first to react to any thought or feeling. It is the mode of mind developed to help you survive. It is very auto-matic. It is based in the reflex to survive. It asks, "How will this harm me? What is wrong? How do I protect my self? What will the loss be?"

The Positive Mind is expansive and practical. It searches for pleasures, for fulfillment, for the possibilities to utilize anything that you experience. It is constructive, risk taking, and active. It examines every thought and feeling for resources to do what you want. It asks, "How is this useful to me? How can this help? What can I do with this? Do I want this? What will this bring me? How far can I go with this?"

The Neutral Mind assesses everything. It is non-attached and never reacts. The Neutral Mind observes the actions of both the Negative and Positive Minds, and then judges both in relationship to your higher self. It takes in all the positive and negative factors and weighs them against your real purpose in the light of your higher self. It asks, "Is this real? Does this support my goal or purpose? What is my mission and vision? Is this meaningful? What is the implication, consequences, and intention?"

Together this trinity of mental functions evaluates everything in terms of the individual identity and ego. It evaluates each thought and perception. Ideally each thought filters through the Negative, the Positive, and then the Neutral Mind. But each individual has one mind stronger than the others. Some thoughts get stuck only in the Negative Mind. Some are passed through to the Positive Mind and expanded without being assessed by the Neutral Mind. Some people have a stronger Negative Mind, or a stronger Positive Mind, or a stronger Neutral Mind. Occasionally, all three are strong and exist in co-equal balance. This is the enlightened mind. It is flexible, creative, and able to reflect the uniqueness of the soul.

Our ability to form emotional judgements is almost instantaneous. A recent brain study showed that we judge a sound, whether we like it or not, in less than 200 thousandths of a second. The sound can be a nonsense syllable, with no obvious reason for liking it or not. Nonetheless, the mind has imme-diate judgements and feelings about the sounds. It is an unconscious process.

That is how fast the Negative and Positive Minds react. Each person can have one of these minds much stronger or weaker than the others. When they all work together you have a powerful instrument to evaluate things and act intelligently on them. The mind used the least and that needs the most development is the Neutral Mind.

Look at the table, **The 81 Facets of the Mind,** which you'll find at the end of this chapter. You can follow how each part of the mind is generated. First see the Functional Minds on the left. These three Functional Minds combine with the three Impersonal Minds, *buddhi, ahangkar,* and *manas,* to give us an emotional and mental stance toward the world. Each combination is called an Aspect. Three Functional Minds times 3 Impersonal Minds gives us 9 Aspects. Think of the Aspect as a stance, a persona, a mental temperament, or an archetype. Your stance might be that of an artist or a leader. All nine are listed in the table. We need them all. We use some Aspects more than others in each circumstance to become a master of that circumstance. We tend to be stronger in one Aspect than another.

You will have a reaction to your own stance. Your minds evaluate what attitude the Aspect should project. The three Functional Minds interact with the 9 Aspects. This generates 27 Controlling Projections. Each of these is listed in the table with a name and a Guiding Phrase. The Meditation Guide (Chapter 13) has a fuller description of the qualities of the Controlling Projections.

There is one last step to generate the Facets. Your mind evaluates how to deliver your attitude. Your Projection goes into an action biased by the evaluation of the Negative, Positive, and Neutral Minds. Three Functional Minds times 27 Projections gives us 81 Facets. Think of the Facets like habits. They are a final readiness to act in a particular way. To run away, be still, or fight. In the table they are indicated with a "-", "+," or "=" to indicate which Functional Mind is dominant and, thereby determines the final Facet and habit. Each Facet is effectively controlled if you strengthen and balance the Projection related to the three Facets.

Aspect	Controlling Projection	Facet
Stance, Persona	Attitude	Action, Habits

The relationships between all these parts of the mind have been summarized graphically in the diagram **How the 9 Aspects, 27 Projections, and 81 Facets Are Generated,** which you will find at the end of this book. The most subtle and intangible are at the top and the most earthy are at the very bottom.

You can see how the qualities in the actions of the Facets derive from the Projections from this table below:

The Characteristics of the Facets
A Controlling Projection interacts with the 3 Functional Minds
to generate 3 Facets

("-") Facet	("+") Facet	("=") Facet
Defensive & protective action	Proactive & pragmatic action	Comprehensive & neutral action
Facets: 1,4,7,10,13,16,19,22,	Facets: 2,5,8,11,14,17,20,23,26,	Facets: 3,6,9,12,15,18,21,24,27,
25,28,31,34,37,40,43,46,49,52,	29,32,35,38,41,44,47,50,53,56,	30,33,36,39,42,45,48,51,54,57,
55,58,61,64,67,70,73,76,79	59,62,65,68,71,74,77,80	60,63,66,69,72,75,78,81

When your mind is refined and balanced, it becomes powerful and it uses each of these Aspects and Projections in a fluid manner. Your mind uses them just like a good musician uses the keys on a piano to produce beautiful music appropriate to the occasion. To work well, each Aspect and Projection must be strong. The power of the mind depends on the strength of each of its parts. You can see in the diagram that each Aspect is supported by and supports three Projections. Each Projection supports and is supported by three Facets.

Many things can go out of balance in this complex system of interactions. It is not a rigid mechanical system. Even though we put this on a diagram to create a map, remember that every atom of the mind and body has its own intelligence as part of the greater Oneness. So what you do, what you say, and what habits you have affect, shape, and rewrite this network. The strength of each connection and which parts work together change and evolve as you do. Your fate and karma are recorded in this network to give you certain talents and certain shortcomings. These are affected by your upbringing, your nutrition, and your relationships. But you have the ability to rewrite the impact of that fate in order to have a new destiny.

It will help you to quickly understand this structure and how to apply it if you trace the connections down one branch of the diagram, **How the 9 Aspects, 27 Projection, and 81 Facets are Generated** inserted at the end of this book.

Look at the diagram and locate the Negative Mind. Notice how this mind sends three branches downward corresponding to the interaction with one of the Impersonal Minds. Follow it down to Aspect #1—the Defender. Here is where the mind takes a stance that is alert and defends you from harm. If you go to the Meditation Guide and look up the Defender Aspect *[page 156]*. The description is:

> "This Aspect looks at everything based on how it may affect you. How will it hurt me or direct me away from what I am trying to do? It defends. The *manas* influence means things seem to come from outside, from impressions of the senses. It is a practical sequence-oriented mental pattern. It wants to know how to deal with it now. What is the action needed? Is it a personal threat, directed at you, or an accident with errors you can correct, or a pure act of nature and coincidence? In each case a different projection is used to deal with it."

The positive power of this Aspect is to shield and defend you on all sides. It is essential in survival situations, yet inappropriate if you over-react and fail to see the situation as it really is. Some may take this stance and live it like a guiding metaphor. They are always aware of what can go wrong and spend a significant energy to become strong and survival equipped. This will be true whether it is a physical or emotional area of life. Without it strong, you are at risk. Too strong, and you can miss the benefits of the other Aspects.

Notice that this Aspect is connected to three Projections further down the diagram. If the Aspect is balanced and strong, it will help regulate those Projections and it will serve the core self or soul. Meditations that adjust the Aspects of your mind are called Core Alignment Meditations, or *antar dhyan*.

Now look at the three Projections that come from the Aspect Defender—Soldier, Ombudsman, and Prospector. Each of these is an attitude that completes and supports the Aspect. These three Projections develop the attitude and skills related to defending you against a threat (#1), an accident (#2), and a coincidence (#3). Each of these attitudes will lead you to behave and feel differently about the same circumstance. If all three are strong and balanced and all three Functional Minds work together, your Defender will be perfect. Unbeatable. Most of us will develop one Projection more than another.

Look more closely at Projection #1—The Soldier. It is generated by *manas* plus two doses of the Negative Mind. It assumes everything is out there—foreign or from another domain. It has little insight about internal processes or blocks that arise from your own emotions. But it is the Projection you want when the enemy is external and real. It mobilizes, focuses, and alerts you. In the Meditation Guide *[page 157]* the description reads:

"This Projection comes from the Negative Mind. It assumes you are personally at risk. Whatever challenges you does so with you as an intentional target."

Its strength is to respond with action regardless of the obstacle or chances. It relies on fearlessness and duty. Compare this to Projection #3—the Prospector. The Prospector is influenced by the Neutral Mind. It looks below the surface of things and knows clearly your purpose. So it may use an apparent loss or an enemy to create a longer-term success or alliance. If it is too dominant when you have a violent threat, you may wait too long to respond. If it does not function at all, you may find many more enemies that are not really enemies but missed opportunities. The description in the Meditation Guide *[page 159]* reads:

"If you know your purpose and goal, you can prospect for what is useful and what is not. Every coincidence is a larger pattern in action. Relax and see beyond the surface to catch useful currents and be in the best position to act intelligently."

If this Projection is weak you may deny your larger sense of Self.

Notice how the skills and qualities associated with each Projection complement each other. Together the three Projections form a stable, complete base for the Aspect to function with. That is why you want all of them strong and balanced in their ability to respond to a challenge and problem in an integrated manner. The Core Alignment Meditations will help the three Projections coordinate with each other as it strengthens the Aspect. To work more directly on Projections, we use a Synchronization Meditation, *patantar pratyahaar*. Look in the diagram. Each Projection is supported by and acts through three Facets. The Facets are the actions and direction of actions with a final spin from the judgements of the three Functional Minds about the Projection and its potential impacts. The word *patantar* means the path of the Projection of a thought through time and space. It is the thread woven through time and space when we choose a direction of action and act. *Pratyahaar* is the action of synchronizing a small part to the whole, the finite to the Infinite. It is synchronizing one action to the Projection of the path of your destiny. So, a meditation applied to the Projection synchronizes the three Facets that connect to it and lead to habits and styles of action. It also strengthens the Controlling Projection itself.

Look on the diagram at the three Facets that are generated from Projection #1—the Soldier. Each Facet comes from the dominant interaction of one of the three Functional Minds. The Soldier attitude may act through any one or a combination of three action pathways—defensively, aggressively, or neutrally. You might divert your enemies, or challenge them to a fight, or decide to form a treaty to use part of their strength and neutralize their harmful intent.

Look at Facet #1. It is an action or orientation to an action that uses the strength of the Negative Mind. It will be a defensive or protective action. For the Soldier this means you may choose to divert an enemy, escape, or prepare yourself with the maximum defensive capabilities.

Suppose your bias leads you to use Facet #2. It will be a proactive or pragmatic action. You would respond with more of the Positive Mind and choose to fight or to use the encounter for a purpose thinking that to start the fight will lead to some option or resource you can use.

If your Neutral Mind dominates with your Projection, then you will act through Facet #3. It will be a comprehensive and neutral action. You will respond to the threat by assessing, strategizing, or deciding on appropriate sacrifices for the central mission or purpose. This includes an intuitive process of judgement that perceives the impacts and relative risks and advantages of an action. All three Facets together are strengths that combine to support the first Projection, the Soldier. A great Soldier uses all the Facets so he can respond to a threat with courage and direct actions regardless of the circumstances.

Many of our problems come from Facets that we use habitually without balance from the three minds. These get stored through our actions in the subconscious and the unconscious in the Universal Mind, *chitta*. They automatically cloak a thought and bias us toward a set of actions without the completion of the full process of the Negative, Positive, and Neutral Minds.

Now look at the entire diagram. You can affect the entire mix of the mind's qualities by meditating at the level of the *gunas* to increase the *sattva* or clarity. Increasing *sattva* is like clearing turbid water. Or, you can clean out the storage of patterns and Facets in the subconscious so you flexibly and consciously engage the new situation without being bound to past reactions, traumas, and imaginations. Or, you can identify the behavior and patterns at the level of the Aspects or Projections and develop your mind there. This is the art and science of dealing with the 81 Facets using Humanology.

There are more meditations that work on each area of this diagram than we have listed in the Meditation Guide. The technology in Kundalini Yoga and in the *Siri Guru Granth Sahib* gives us thousands of techniques that allow for sophisticated designs and applications that incorporate every nuance of the personality and the potential problems. This listing is the gateway to a practical psychology of applied meditation techniques.

To get a better sense of the whole structure go through the diagram carefully. Trace each of the branches and see how the Aspects, Projections, and

Facets connect to each other. It will give you many insights about your own patterns, strengths, and weaknesses. Imagine looking at your self when *manas*, the sensory, externally oriented mind is dominant. When have you acted this way? What is your normal pattern? Then imagine what happens when *ahangkar* rules. How would you approach the same situation or relationship? How would you speak and communicate? Do the same for the *buddhi* mind. Work your way through all the branches of the diagram. They are the many branches of your mind.

This is a way to encounter your mind. A way to feel its boundaries, shape, function, and potential. We invite you to explore. Experience your self and share what you learn with others. There are thousands of case examples of how people used these techniques on their own or with a little help from a teacher or mentor. And then they were able to make profound changes where they thought nothing was even possible. There are many people who incorporate some favorite techniques to stay balanced and steady in their lives. This is a good place to begin to explore the territory of your mind. Knowledge of the mind is not intellectual. It is an experienced wisdom that is gained only by personal practice, by a *sadhana*. As you try these techniques remember: you are here just to be you, and your mind is your best servant.

Sat Naam.

The 81 Facets of the Mind

THREE FUNCTIONAL MINDS	ASPECTS FUNCTIONAL MIND X IMPERSONAL MIND	Controlling Projections			81 FACETS
		ASPECT INTERACTING WITH FUNCTIONAL MIND		GUIDING PHRASE	
N E G A T I V E M I N D	Negative Mind X **1** Manas *Defender*	Negative	*Soldier*	How to deal wtih a threat	− + N
		Positive	*Ombudsman*	How to deal with an accident	− + N
		Neutral	*Prospector*	How to deal with a coincidence	− + N
	Negative Mind X **2** Ahangkar *Manager*	Negative	*Historian*	Relay of a past memory	− + N
		Positive	*Chameleon*	Phase of a mental projection	− + N
		Neutral	*Judge*	Shadow of a mental projection	− + N
	Negative Mind X **3** Buddhi *Preserver*	Negative	*Runner*	Deep memory of a past projection	− + N
		Positive	*Integrator*	Mental intersection	− + N
		Neutral	*Apostle*	Mental outer projection	− + N
P O S I T I V E M I N D	Positive Mind X **4** Manas *Artist*	Negative	*Actor*	The Art of memorizing creativity	− + N
		Positive	*Doer*	The Art of creating art	− + N
		Neutral	*Originator*	The Art of creating creativity	− + N
	Positive Mind X **5** Ahangkar *Producer*	Negative	*Gourmet*	Creating art through past memory	− + N
		Positive	*Architect*	Creating art by environmental effects	− + N
		Neutral	*Entrepreneur*	Creating art by projecting into the future	− + N
	Positive Mind X **6** Buddhi *Missionary*	Negative	*Devotee*	Pursuing the cycle of success	− + N
		Positive	*Enthusiast*	Pursuing the cycle of artistic attributes	− + N
		Neutral	*Creator*	Pursuing the art of cohesiveness	− + N
N E U T R A L M I N D	Neutral Mind X **7** Manas *Strategist*	Negative	*Scout*	Judging environments through the senses	− + N
		Positive	*Coach*	Judging environments	− + N
		Neutral	*Guide*	Judging positive environments through intuition	− + N
	Neutral Mind X **8** Ahangkar *Leader*	Negative	*Protector*	Assessment of the position	− + N
		Positive	*Commander*	Assessment of the successful	− + N
		Neutral	*Pathfinder*	Assessment of personality & facets through intuition	− + N
	Neutral Mind X **9** Buddhi *Teacher*	Negative	*Educator*	Intuitive assessment of personality defects to be covered	− + N
		Positive	*Expert*	Interpretations of all facets of life	− + N
		Neutral	*Master*	Assessment of personality of overlords & their projections to be controlled	− + N

13 Meditation Guide

How to Use
the Meditation Guide

N OW THAT YOU KNOW HOW THE 81 FACETS, 27 PROJECTIONS, AND 9 Aspects are generated, you have two ways to approach the development and understanding of the mind, top down or bottom up. From the top of the big cosmic map going downward, you can refine and balance the foundations of the mind. You can affect the *gunas* and refine the substance of the *chitta*. You can balance the expression of the *tattvas* and strengthen each of your three Functional Minds. This will affect your entire mental disposition and functioning. It will have a cascade effect throughout the network of your mind and personality. The first six meditations in this guide help develop each of these parts of your mind.

You can also approach the mind from the bottom up. You can notice your personality patterns, perceptual habits, and impulses. You can look at the traits of your body and read the elements that are dominant in it. You can analyze the qualities in your language and voice to find the way you project in any situation. You can analyze how you react under stress. Under stress you fall back on your most exaggerated strengths and act out unconsciously your weakest or most unbalanced parts. Then you can use a Synchronization Meditation to add flexibility to those habits, to awaken strengths and resources within you, and to empty the subconscious of the many fears and habits that block you.

In a healthy mind each Aspect aligns itself with you, with your core personality. The meditation for each Aspect strengthens the qualities of that Aspect and connects it in a balanced way to your core. These meditations are called Core Alignment Meditations, or *antar dhyan*. When it is aligned, each Aspect contributes the talent and perceptions that come from its stance to support your awareness, your central purpose and the intention of your soul. Practice of the correctly chosen Core Alignment Meditation produces profound shifts in the practitioner.

Each Projection is an important link between the Aspect and the final direction of action and habit in the Facets. The Projections also need balance, so they are neither too strong nor too weak for your task. For each Projection there is a meditation technique specifically targeting it. These are called Synchronizing Meditations, or *patantar pratyahaar*. They synchronize two things: the Projection itself to support the Aspect and the three Facets to support the Projection. There are other ways to treat and change the Facets directly, but adjusting them from the level of the Projection is much more effective and lasting. It changes the matrix of the mind it is in, as well as the Facet itself.

To learn this system and see how powerful it can be, read through the guide carefully. Then identify an area in yourself you would like to refine or change. Choose that meditation and do it for 40 days. Experience this yourself.

The duration of 40 days of practice is chosen to let the meditation provoke your subconscious to release any thoughts and emotional patterns that hinder you. The *chitta* stores all the memories, sensory impressions, and the patterns created in the Facets. A good meditation will break your old patterns, put in a seed for a new pattern, and clear out the subconscious.

Unlike some approaches to the use of meditation, we use the full power and range of sound and language. Language is one of the main reasons that we have larger and more complex brains than our nearest simian relatives. The ability to search for meaning and to sense intuition and subtlety in complex patterns required our brain growth. The use of language and sound is a powerful tool for change. It is integrated into our very cells and neurons. Sound can activate the glands, change the way we think, and alter the deep subconscious.

Many meditations use language combined with rhythm and a special quality called *naad. Naad* is an energetic template formed in the root elements of a language. It makes sound penetrate, creates deep shifts in feeling, and opens intuition. We use sounds, mantra, and a special form of mantra called *shabd* to break, reorganize, and refine the ego. We use *shabd* to open our perception and relationship to the core self. A great source for this special catalytic language is from the Sikh tradition in *the Siri Guru Granth Sahib.* It is a source for universal sounds that capture the dance of the mind, move you to dwell in vastness, and move you to drop your neuroses and fears. It belongs to everyone. It is a treasure chest of gems for your mind. Those secrets that were discovered and left as a legacy by the Gurus are for this time. They are to serve the awakening of humanity as we mature into the new age and expand into space. In this space age, we need to rely on our awareness, our intelligence, our intuition, and our compassion. The disciplines that give that are in Kundalini Yoga. The psychology that applies it is Humanology.

You will find the range and variety of meditation techniques contained in this meditation guide extraordinary. This legacy is ideal for tailoring to specific applications. We have used these techniques to build the business performance of executives, to reduce stress, to eliminate addictions, to enhance health and immune fitness, to instill intelligence in children, and to improve athletic performance. These techniques have been used to increase longevity, memory, vitality, and sexual potency. Millions of people are using these techniques and benefiting. These techniques are a necessary part of a healthy lifestyle. These meditations and your discipline promise a grand partnership and a way to touch the whole human being—body, mind, and spirit.

First Steps:
Meditation for
Absolute Beginners

MEDITATION IS EVERYWHERE. IN THE MEDIA, IN HOSPITALS AND CLINICS, in exercise programs, on athletic fields, and even in the boardrooms of the corporate world. Something which seemed so foreign and strange only 20 years ago is now everywhere. Many of us have still not tried it. We have heard about it; seen it demonstrated by someone. We have an idea about it but wonder how to begin. How can I know without trying it, if it is worth the effort, if it is really for me, if it will help, and if I will be any good at it?

Relax. Rest assured that meditation is for everyone. It is just like a daily shower to clean the body. It cleans the mind. It helps you avoid mistakes, focus your energy, stay healthy, and become kind and prayerful in your heart. It is not magic. It is not religion. It is a technology that uses what you already have—your senses, your mind, and your body. It just uses a few refined patterns to create a communication between you and your mind and between your mind and your body.

A morning or evening practice of meditation and Kundalini Yoga is the only thing I know that generates time. Time is the most common complaint I hear. Where is the time to do something good for my self? Where is the time to meditate? The answer is meditation gives you time back in multiples of what you put in to it. How? We waste a tremendous amount of time by losing our focus on what is really important. Meditation hones that focus. We also make mistakes because our mind drifts and becomes unconscious with daydreams and with unintentional thoughts. Meditation clears the subconscious and helps you keep your clarity. It lets you be present to what you are doing. We also lose time because we do not see resources and opportunities that are already present. We narrow our view under stress and pressure. Meditation integrates the broad lens of the mind with the narrow focus of action. So there are many ways that time is saved as you go through your day alert, energized, and victorious.

The Meditation Experience

The specific feelings and thoughts you experience when you meditate are yours alone. Each person will be different according to background, mental temperament, depth, and type of meditation. It is ultimately a private act even when you meditate in a group. Generally when you begin to draw your attention inward and stop the normal outward focus of your attention, you will become aware of what else is going on in the background. Just like being quiet lets you hear the sounds of nature from outside your office or home. That may be pleasant or unsettling depending on what is in the background. But as you sit and learn to slow your breath and be relaxed, even the unsettling things can be watched with equanimity. You can quickly become comfortable processing all kinds of feelings and thoughts. When you go more deeply into a sound or a focus, the subconscious that is filled with thoughts and feelings dumps itself. When that dump occurs you may wonder what is happening. Nothing. It is just like cleaning out an old closet. Some things are still useful, and you can keep them; others are long outdated, and you toss them. Soon you have more room to take in life and more room to think and feel your own self, rather than all the subconscious clutter. The mind never stops. But you can create a stillness within you where you do not react to the mind. This stillness often calms the flow of the mind and creates a quiet spot in the center of the storm. This rejuvenates and relaxes almost everyone who experiences it.

A Place to Meditate

Any place you can be undisturbed for a while is a good place to meditate. Choose a spot that is not too cool and not too hot. Put something supportive but soft under you to sit on. Most practitioners use a sheepskin, or a blanket. Many prefer a wool or cotton one. If they are stiff, some people find it comfortable to have a firm pillow, 4 to 6 inches high, under the buttocks to take away any pressure from the lower spine. If you cannot sit comfortably cross-legged on the floor, then sit in a chair. The only condition is to be sure that your weight is equally distributed on both feet. We want the spine to be erect and reasonably straight. It acts like a central channel for the energy of your nervous system. Many people create a special spot. A "power spot" or sacred place. They think of meditation as a process to calm the mind and then help them to sit very clearly with their spirit. So the meditation spot has some objects that uplift them and remind them of their spirit or of nature.

Many people are finding it useful to meditate while at work. They use these techniques to shift their mind out of a rut. They use meditation to become clear and to communicate with others better. Some use it to handle stress or to create rapport with team members.

While driving you should not meditate, just drive. Breathing meditations can distract you or make you a little spacey if you are not used to them, just drive. You might play meditation music on the car stereo. Many people like to do that so they are relaxed or prepared for action when they arrive.

A Good Time to Meditate

Any time when you are alert and ready to try it is good. Advanced meditators prefer the morning hours, especially the time between 4 a.m. and 8 a.m. The 2-1/2 hours before the rise of the sun are even called the nectar hours. At that early time nothing else is going on. Instead of having many dreams, you meditate and clear your own mind. It is also the time all of nature wakes up and activates.

Many people like to meditate for a while before sleep. It clears the worries and business of the day and lets you go into deep sleep quickly, allowing you to build your reserve energies for the new day. It is a good rule to not meditate after a big meal. After all, the blood is all in your stomach, and there is little for your brain.

Length of Time of Meditations

Each meditation works on different parts of your mind and body. The time varies with the technique. There are meditations that have a great impact and that take anywhere from 3 minutes up to 2-1/2 hours. The common times used for a significant effect from a practice are: 11 minutes, 15 minutes, 22 minutes, 31 minutes, 62 minutes, 1-1/2 hours, 2-1/2 hours. Most of the meditations in this guide are 11 to 31 minutes. To begin with try only what is comfortable. Even 5 minutes will bring you benefits. The first benefit is to simply stop your automatic routine, your unconscious patterns where you rush through life and do not even note that you are alive.

The Right Meditation

The guide has 42 meditations. Pick one that seems not too difficult and that matches your pattern. Ultimately there are no wrong ones. There are only more right ones. If you have never done any meditation at all, then try the beginner's meditation at the end of this section, and then go from there. You can also pick up a beginner's tape that guides you through the first steps. The best will be a tape that gives you some exercise first as preparation, and then a deep meditation.

No Longer Secret

These meditations were once a secret. Yogi Bhajan has openly taught these techniques from Kundalini Yoga to everyone beginning in 1969. He declared that secret initiations in this yoga were for the past. It is the Aquarian Age and these techniques belong to everyone. They are a science and need to be shared and tested for the benefit of all. Now you can get the techniques in books like this, on the Internet, and from 3HO Kundalini Yoga centers on every continent and in most countries around the world.

Diet and Health

The recommended diet for meditators is to eat lightly and with health in mind. It is true that many meditators have become vegetarian for health reasons. They choose the lightest diet that lets the mind be calm and focused. Lowering all the protein and acidity from meat helps. There are some meditations, especially used in healing that are accompanied by a special diet to work on some gland or organ in the body. But meditation as a general technique has no requirements that way. You are requested to not take any drugs. Medicine is excepted. LSD, marijuana, amphetamines, and other psychoactive compounds may imbalance you.

Meditation is not harmful if you follow instructions. Whenever there is a breathing pattern be sure to do it correctly. The breath is a powerful force in the body and needs to be done correctly just as in any sport or exercise. If you have any question about your capacity to do simple exercises or sitting, see your doctor for a check-up first.

The Use of Sounds

Real silence is the goal of many techniques. But real silence is when the ego is quiet. It is when you can hear your own self above the chatter of your mind. You may not speak out loud for years but still have a huge clamor inside.

Meditations often use sounds. Sometimes they are simple sounds, like a do-re-mi for the mind. When you use basic sounds with rhythm it penetrates the mind, and it redirects the flow of thoughts so something new can come in. Sometimes words like Love, Beauty, Truth, or even God are used. They are always big thoughts. Thoughts that break our narrow confines and our fears and elevate us. The words come from many traditions. They can be in many languages. A mantra in English is " I am, I AM." It can be used in German as "Ich Bin, ICH BIN." Many of the words used in well-tested classical meditations are from Punjabi or Sanskrit. These are languages made up in ancient times, of primary sounds for the purpose of meditation. They are still effective today, for they are timeless syllables. What is needed are words you do not make up, because you want to go beyond your own patterns, affirmations, and confirmations. What is needed are sounds or words that give you a taste of the state you want to dwell in.

Someone always asks if meditation is a religion or a belief. It is not a religion. It does admit you are body, mind, and spirit. But it clears the mind, pure and simple. This lets you bring more energy and spirit to whatever your tradition or religion may be. You can practice it as a human, even as an atheist. It is about human capacity and the relationship to your mind and whole self. It doesn't give you some specific belief. It does make you more believable about your beliefs.

Do any of the words used mean that we are chanting to some god that we don't know? No. You are chanting in your mind to evoke a state or to feel your own sacredness and soul. There is no concept at all of "chanting to someone." It is an energetic act that changes your brain, stimulates hormone balance, and engages you in a special conversation with your own mind about vastness and truth.

Some cultures are used to using sounds, singing in public, and addressing their own mind. Others are more reticent and private with sounds. The yogi is free to use all of the senses in meditation: sight, touch, sound, and even smell. You will find many silent meditations, many with sounds used mentally, and many with sounds repeated out loud. It all depends on the effect and impact you want to produce.

The Use of Breath

Many meditations use the breath as part of the technique. Some meditations require you to simply shift your attention to the flow of the breath. Breath is your life. Its depth, rate, and pattern are correlated with your moods and level of energy, so the breath can be used to change them. Some meditations control the breath in specific patterns: by regulating the ratio of the inhale and exhale; by breaking the inhale or exhale into segments; by changing the speed of the breath; or by using mantra.

Whenever you use the breath be sure to follow the instructions carefully and ask an instructor if you have any questions. Begin the practice of a breath meditation for a short time and gradually increase the length as you accommodate to the changes it induces. If you ever feel dizzy when using the breath, stop and be sure you are using proper technique, have not taken any drugs, and are not sick. When used rightly, breath meditations create a lot of change and you feel comfortable, as well as balanced.

Check to be sure you normally breathe with a complete breath pattern: begin the inhale by letting the belly relax and go out, then fill the middle chest, then finally the upper chest. Exhale by letting the upper chest deflate, then empty the central chest, and finally pull the navel point into expel the last bit of breath. This is the normal pattern of breath when you are healthy and breathe correctly.

About 30 percent of people do not breathe correctly. So check your breathing pattern by holding one hand over your belly and one in the center of your chest to observe yourself breathing. If you learned incorrectly, it is easy to change and will have a profound positive impact on your vitality, metabolism, and moods. Unless otherwise specified in the meditations in the guide, breathing is through the nose.

How to Dress

Dress any way you like that is comfortable and nonrestrictive. There are three considerations when you think about dress. The first is simple comfort, so you can relax and freely do any exercises associated with your routine. Second is sacredness. Many people think of meditation as a special time, as a time to put themselves in front of the mind, consciousness, and soul. So the clothes are clean, fresh, and often light in color and composition. Third is subtle energetics. Meditators who have become very sensitive to the subtle currents of energy in the body report sensing channels of energy called meridians and centers of energy called chakras. They noticed that meditation is helped by letting the hair grow, since the hair acts like antennae for etheric and solar energy to enter the body. To maximize this source of energy you may see traditions that curl the hair on top of the head. That was called the "*rishi* knot" or the "knot of the wise ones." They would also cover the head with something cotton. That is why you see prayer shawls, turbans, yarmulkes, and other ways to put a cotton filter over the chakra at the top of the head. It is not required, but evolved from the sensitivity and sophistication of regular practitioners.

A Beginner's Meditation

Here are three techniques to get you started.

1. Sit with a straight spine. Sit either in a chair or in a comfortable cross-legged position on a mat or sheepskin. Let your hands relax in your lap. Rest the back of the right hand into the up-turned palm of the left hand. Keep the shoulders relaxed and the upper chest slightly lifted to support your spine and to create balance. Keep your eyes 9/10ths closed. They are slightly open to let in a little light.

Now turn your attention to the flow of your breath. Breathe only through the nose. At first just watch it. Feel every bit of the sensation of inhaling, exhaling, and all the movements. You can feel your entire body reflect the motion of breathing in little ways. After 2 or 3 minutes, begin to consciously slow the breath down. Your normal breathing rate is 14 to 17 breaths a minute. As you watch the breath, slow it to 8 times a minute or less—4 times a minute is excellent. Hear the slight sound the breath makes as it goes in and out.

Let all the thoughts just come and go. They are like background noises from people at a party. You have invited all the parts of your mind to enjoy this moment. Let all those thoughts go. You stay with the flow and feeling of the breath. Do this for another 6 to 8 minutes. Then end, with a deep inhale, exhale, and finally inhale as you stretch both arms up toward the ceiling. Now relax.

2. Take the same position as above. This time roll your eyes up gently. Focus through the point on the brow between the eyebrows and above the top of the nose. This is called the brow point. When you focus there it brings your thoughts into an automatic coherence, and it engages your higher glands to support your meditation effort. Through the brow, imagine a blue sky. Feel as if you could fly freely in the ethers. Slow the breath down.

Now add a mental affirmation. As you breathe in and as you breathe out mentally repeat this phrase: "Bountiful, Blissful, and Beautiful I am." Say it mentally as many times as it takes to match the length of your breath. It might be one to four repetitions. As you say each word mentally feel what it means. Project this thought with your mind. If the mind wanders and starts to jump or object, just notice that and let the affirmation run through the middle of that thought. Lift all the other thoughts off to Infinity with this affirmation. Don't try to stop the other thoughts, just return to this affirmation. Do this for 11 minutes. Then inhale deeply and relax.

3. Take the same position. Focus at the brow point. Now let's try a sound. Take a deep breath. A deep breath starts to go in at the belly or navel. Then it fills the middle chest then the upper. As you exhale, let the air go from the top of the chest. Slowly pull in the belly as the last breath goes out. After a few deep breaths to center yourself, relax, inhale deeply and project this sound— **Saa-a-a-a-a-a**. It is a long continuous sound, rhyming with the "bu" in "but." Raise the pitch just enough so you can feel the vibration of the sound at the brow point on the forehead where you are focusing your attention. It will feel like a little massage or pressure. It will be pleasant. Project the sound as if you are sending a message to a far-off hill. When you run out of breath, inhale slowly and deeply. Begin again. Continue 3 to 11 minutes. Then inhale deeply, hold the breath in for 10 seconds. Then relax the breath and sit very still for another minute. Observe your own mind, your energy, and your feelings. This sound is very "open." It resonates as you say it. It is a basic sound, a phoneme. It is not a word. But it does have an energy and feeling associated with it. It will make you feel calm and vast. The yogis associated the feeling of totality and the entire cosmos with it. So, when you create this tone you can enhance it by extending your feeling and the imagination with this sound to the entire cosmos in all directions. Let your mind meditate beyond the horizon in all directions for a few minutes.

You are all set to go. Explore these teachings. Check with the resource sites for more information and training if you like. Take a little time to get one step ahead of Time.

The Meditations

MEDITATION TO ENRICH THE MIND

Sit with your spine straight. Put the right hand palm up and the left hand with palm down. Put the elbows by the sides and lift the hands up to the level of the heart center. Do not let the hands hang loosely or without balance. Hold both hands steadily. Close your eyes.

Chant with the tape "Pavan, Pavan" by Gurushabd Singh Khalsa.

Pavan pavan pavan pavan para paraa pavan guroo,
Pavan guroo whaa-hay guroo whaa-hay guroo pavan guroo.

The air, the air, the air, the air. The Infinity and beyond the Infinity.
The air is the Guru.
The air is the Guru. Wha! The Guru is beyond description.
Wha! The Guru is wonderful. The air is the Guru.

Be sure to use the tip of the tongue distinctly. Continue for 31 minutes. Then inhale, hold the breath for 10-15 seconds. Concentrate on your hands. Then bring your hands together and exhale. Inhale deeply in the original posture. Hold the breath and stretch your spine upwards. After 10-15 seconds exhale strongly. One more time, inhale deeply. Stretch your spine totally. Keep the chin in, chest out. After 10-20 seconds exhale through the mouth powerfully. Relax.

MEDITATION FOR THE SATTVIC GUNA

Listening to Angelic Whispers

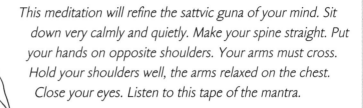

This meditation will refine the sattvic guna of your mind. Sit down very calmly and quietly. Make your spine straight. Put your hands on opposite shoulders. Your arms must cross. Hold your shoulders well, the arms relaxed on the chest. Close your eyes. Listen to this tape of the mantra.

**Ardaas bhayee, amar daas guroo,
Amar daas guroo, ardaas bhayee,
Raam daas guroo, raam daas guroo,
Raam daas guroo, sachee sahee.**

The Grace of Guru Amar Das (who is the Hope of the hopeless) and Guru Ram Das (who is the King of the yogis and Bestower of blessings—past, present, and future) guarantee the prayer will be answered and all one's needs provided for.

As you listen to the instruments play this tune, whistle with it. Hear the sound of the whistle at the brow point. Keep the eyes closed. Inside of your self, be very calm, quiet. This is a posture of peace. Continue 15-31 minutes. Then begin long, slow, deep breathing. Mentally listen to the echo of your whistling. Hear the sound you created before. Bring your unison power of the mind, the subtle sattvic guna of the mind, to listen. Once you learn to listen this way, you can listen in exactly the same way to what God's Will is. When you can still the mind, refine it, command its guna, then you can listen to God's Will, discern what it is, then act. Life will be very easy, content, and fulfilled. In the Bible you are told the same thing. There is a word called "Behold." Behold yourself. Be within yourself and listen.

Continue for 3 to 11 minutes.

End with three powerful breaths: inhale deep through the nose, hold for 5-10 seconds, then exhale powerfully through the mouth. As you hold the breath in, put all the pressure downward on your shoulders with your hands. Press them down, and keep the spine steady and straight. Repeat the breath three times. Then relax.

MEDITATION TO COMMAND
YOUR FIVE TATTVAS

This mantra meditation from the Siri Guru Granth Sahib is a gift to you that will let you penetrate into the unknown without fear. It will give you protection and mental balance.

Sit very straight. Listen to a tape of this mantra:

Aap sahaaee hoaa
Sachay daa sachaa doaa
Har, har, har

The Lord Himself has become our protector,
the Truest of the True has taken care of us.
God, God, God.

When you hear the word **Har**, pull the navel point in. For the three words of **Har**, your breath will become a 3-stroke breath of fire. Then suspend the breath out as you keep the navel point pulled in and listen to the rest of the mantra. Just before the **Har** sounds come again, inhale quickly and repeat the breath stroke cycle again.

To use the Naad and imprint your mind, do this meditation each day for 62 minutes. Do it for 90 days. Then you will know the practical experience and power and miracle of the spoken word.

It is very simple and rhythmic. If you do it very nobly it will be extremely helpful. Whenever you are effective and create a success in your life, you also must generate some opposition and animosity. That is called the Law of Polarity. It is called facing a square in your life. This meditation will totally eliminate enemies and block the impact of animosity forever. It can give you mental self-control and let you command your five tattvas for effective living.

MEDITATION FOR THE NEGATIVE MIND

When you need to balance the flashing negativity and protective fervor of the Negative Mind, use this meditation. It clears the subconscious of unwanted negative or fearful thoughts. Then the Negative Mind can give you clear signals to protect and to promote you. The posture is one of calmness and humility that lets the Creator, the Unknown, cover and shield you. This used to be called Beggar's Posture.

Sit straight in an easy cross-legged pose. Make a cup of the two hands with both palms facing up, and the right hand resting on top of the left hand. The fingers will cross over each other. Put this open cup at the level of the heart center. Elbows rare elaxed at the sides. Your eyes are slightly open and look down toward the hands.

Inhale deeply in a long steady stroke through the nose. Exhale in a focused stream through rounded lips. You will feel the breath go over the hands. Let any thought or desire that is negative, or persistently distracting come into your mind as you breathe. Breathe the thought and feeling in, and exhale it out with the breath.

After 11 to 31 minutes, exhale completely and suspend the breath out as you lock in the navel point. Concentrate on each vertebra of the spine until you can feel it all the way to the base, as stiff as a rod. Then inhale powerfully, exhale completely, and repeat the concentration. Repeat this final breath 3-5 times. Then relax completely.

The length of time is 11 to 31 minutes.

MEDITATION FOR THE POSITIVE MIND

This practice opens the heart center and the feelings of the positive self. It is a gesture of happiness. It has a great history and is said to have been practiced by many great and wise spiritual leaders including Buddha and Christ. The hand mudra became a symbol for blessing and prosperity.

Sit with an erect spine. Curl the ring finger and little finger into each palm. Bend the thumbs over top of them to lock them into place. Keep the first two fingers straight. Bring the arms so the elbows are by the sides, and the hands are by the shoulders with the two fingers of each hand pointing straight up. Bring the forearms and hands forward to an angle of 30 degrees from the vertical. Press the shoulders and elbows back firmly but comfortably. The palms face forward. Close the eyelids. Roll the eyes up gently and concentrate at the brow point—the Third Eye area—at the top of the nose where the eyebrows would meet. Create a steady, slow, deep, and complete breath. Mentally pulse rhythmically from the brow point out to Infinity the sounds:

Saa taa naa maa

Saa *is Infinity.* **Taa** *is Life.* **Naa** *is Death.* **Maa** *is Rebirth/Transformation.*

This describes the cycle of life. This kriya brings a total mental balance to the psyche. The entire mantra means, "I meditate on Truth, Truth that I am."

Try it for 40 days. During that time eat lightly and speak only truth directly from your heart. Practice for 11 to 62 minutes.

To end the meditation, inhale deeply and exhale three times. Then open and close the fists several times. Relax.

MEDITATION FOR THE NEUTRAL MIND

It is easy to hear a truth and difficult to live it, to embed it deeply into your heart and mind. The Neutral Mind opens the gate to that deep remembrance of the self and soul. Jappa done with the refined Neutral Mind leads to Naam chit aveh. The Neutral Mind lives for the touch of vastness. It lets all other thoughts be without disturbance to your constant inner light.

Sit in easy pose with the spine straight. Put both hands in the lap with the palms facing up. Rest the right hand into the left. The thumb tips may touch or not. Remove all tension from every part of the body. Sit straight by achieving a balance. Close the eyes. Imagine seeing your self sitting peacefully and full of radiance. Then gradually let your energy collect like a flow at the brow point. Let the breath regulate itself into a meditative slow, almost suspended, manner. Concentrate without effort at that point and mentally vibrate in a simple monotone, as if chopping the sound, projecting each syllable distinctly:

Wha-hay gu-roo

Infinity identity from darkness to light.

Call on the higher self and keep going steadily through all barriers. Let go and let God.

Practice this meditation for 11 to 31 minutes at a session.

Negative Mind x Manas

Qualities: *This Aspect looks at everything based on how it may affect you. How will it hurt me or direct me away from what I am trying to do? It defends. The manas influence means things seem to come from outside, from impressions of the senses. It is a practical sequence-oriented mental pattern. It wants to know how to deal with it now. What is the action needed? Is it a personal threat, directed at you, or an accident with errors you can correct, or a pure act of nature and coincidence? In each case a different Projection is called on to deal with it. When this is* **too strong,** *you may appear to be rigid, reactive, and over-dominant. You fail to see your own contribution to the situation and react quickly but without detailed assessment for long-term implications. You will also be very self-critical about your performance. If this is* **too weak** *or underdeveloped, you lack survival instincts that defend you against the ill motives of others; you become victim to situations where your efforts will not have beneficial reciprocity; and you lack the level of detail-checking that prevents errors before they happen. When* **balanced** *you deliver strong focused actions that enjoy challenge. You act, but always with a cover and a back-up plan. The Soldier gives you quick action, the Ombudsman gives you versatility and pragmatic solutions, and the Prospector lets you move opportunistically to your own advantage. When all three Projections are balanced they support the function of the Aspect to align with your real purpose and to see things as they are.*

Core Alignment Meditation

Sit straight and focus at the brow point. Hands on knees in gian mudra. Chant this mantra:

Gobinday	*Sustains You*
Mukanday	*Liberates You*
Udaaray	*Elevates You*
Apaaray	*Delivers You Across*
Hareeang	*Destroys All*
Kareeang	*Creates All*
Nirnaamay	*Beyond Category and Name*
Akaamay	*Beyond Desire*

The mantra is chanted on one breath and takes about 15 seconds. To chant it correctly, inhale deep, pull in the navel, and apply Mul Bandh as you begin to chant. Cinch the Mul Bandh a little tighter with each phrase. Exhale and continue.

Chant for 31 minutes. This meditation works on subconscious blocks, especially around issues of fear.

"How to Deal with a Threat"

Negative Mind x Manas/Negative

This Projection comes from the Negative Mind. It assumes you are personally at risk. Whatever challenges you does so with you as an intentional target. **Too strong** *and it can doubt itself, feel it has not covered the threat enough. So it becomes driven and goes on anxious searches, occasionally relentless inquisitions. It can respond massively to a small threat to make sure there are no survivors to be a threat later.* **Too weak,** *you think threats won't become a real attack or disaster. You require too much evidence and assume dangerous threats are intended for someone else or not intended at all. It is hard to imagine evil intent or ill will. When* **balanced,** *you can respond quickly and fearlessly, regardless of the apparent size of the problem or opposition. You use a single-minded focus on duty and objective, by systematically eliminating everything that doesn't lead to your goal. You are serious and focused. Everything you do or others do around you must move toward your objective and not limit or hurt your position.*

Synchronization Meditation

Sit with a straight spine. Relax arms at the sides with elbows against the ribs. Forearms are parallel to the ground and angled outward to form a 60-degree angle between them. Hands are in closed Lotus Mudra, the finger and thumbs tips all touching, with the fingers and thumbs pointing up. Focus at the brow point. Inhale very deeply and fully. Exhale completely. Lock the breath out. Pull the navel point in. Apply a firm Mul Bandh. As you hold the breath out, repeat mentally in 16 beats:

Saa taa naa maa   Saa taa naa maa
Saa taa naa maa   Saa taa naa maa

Then inhale deeply, and exhale immediately. Continue for 31 minutes.

This meditation takes you beyond all fear and lets the soldier act direct and true.

"How to Deal with an Accident"

Negative Mind x Manas/Positive

Everything just needs a fix-up. Take all the pieces and find what is useful. Find an advantage in this situation. Catalogue what you did wrong so that you won't do the same in the future. Discover what you didn't do that will protect you later. Identify, fix, and use. **Too strong**, *you can get distracted by other people's priorities or opportunities that arise. You can take on jobs not related to your primary task, or overestimate how much change you can affect. If the Positive and Negative Minds interlock, then you can become convinced of your solution from past experience and fix something that is not broken or fix the wrong thing which then creates another problem.* **Too weak**, *you get frustrated in constant attempts to move beyond the problem, since you skip details or don't trust your own instincts to act in a new way. You fiddle instead of fix. You let your effort drift and become distracted without fully testing it. When* **balanced** *and developed, you are a practical, effective, action-oriented learning machine. You notice enough details to act precisely and are confident enough to take proportional risks and test the results by external benchmarks. Great under emergency and panic situations.*

Synchronization Meditation

Brahm Mudra Kriya

Sit straight. Place both hands in front of you at eye level. Extend the Jupiter (index) finger straight up. Curl the other fingers into the palm. Keep the thumbs straight up, parallel to the index finger, thumbnails toward the body. The tip of the left index finger is held at the level of the lowest knuckle of the right thumb. Hands are 6-8 inches apart and about 1 to 1-1/2 feet from the face. The eyes are open, looking straight and directly at and through the space between the hands. Make your breath long and slow.

Continue for 11 to 31 minutes.

"How to Deal with a Coincidence"
Negative Mind x Manas/Neutral

*If you know your purpose and goal, you can prospect for what is useful and what is not. Every coincidence is a larger pattern in action. Relax and see beyond the surface to catch useful currents and be in the best position to act intelligently. **Too strong**, you assess and doubt everything, look under the surface and test everyone for lies and fabrications. You are very loyal but prone to cut corners if you think you understand what is needed and they don't. If this projection is **weak** you may be overly fearful about future consequences of your actions and delay. You can overestimate the power or position of others or the level of intractability of the problem. Under stress you can withdraw into work and many tasks and not give your rich emotions a place for expression, not knowing what consequences they bring. So it is important to have hobbies or areas unrelated to your main job. When **balanced**, you are an excellent financial officer, legal strategist, and cross-examiner. You keep everyone straight and notice things others do not, as you show intelligence and strategic vision capacity.*

Synchronization Meditation

Seven Wave "Sat Naam" Meditation

*Sit straight. Place the palms together at the center of the chest, thumbs touching the center of the sternum. With the eyes closed focus at the brow point. Inhale deeply. With the exhale chant a long **Sat** with a short **Naam**. Vibrate **Sat** in 6 waves, with **Naam** forming the seventh. On each wave, thread the sound up through the chakras beginning at the base of the spine. On **Naam** project the sound through the crown of the head to Infinity. As the sound penetrates each chakra, gently pull the physical area of the body it corresponds to (i.e. rectum, sex organs, navel point, heart, throat, brow point, and crown of the head).*

Sat Nam *means "Your identity is Reality or Truth"*

Continue for 11 to 31 minutes.

This meditation will give you balance and clear intuition.

Negative Mind x Ahangkar

Qualities: *This Aspect defends and preserves the balance of your identity and your projected roles under the pressure of actions, and under the influence of the expectations of others. It actively sets boundaries in relationships. The issue will be insecurity and distrust of appearance of others. It wants to know "What is really going on. What is your intention?"* **Too strong** *and you act rigid in a desperate search for the rules to make order out of everything. Once you have the rules you can manage and act perfectly. You act well at work but harbor a strong resentment if you don't have personal material and security to show for the efforts.* **Too weak,** *you can feel overwhelmed, lose track of the rules, feel the world ignores your priorities, and you become very self-critical and sad. You look around for order rather than starting from your own internal center. Sometimes it has a barrier to joining emotionally. To cope, you may think too much, like the Historian, or shift to please and find order, like the Chameleon, or find hidden patterns that oppose you with your intuition, like the Judge.* **Balanced** *and fully developed, you can reduce conflicts, keep towards the main tasks and mission you took on, and protect your own interests. You are quite capable of delaying pleasure and redirecting impulses in order to reach what is more important to you. You deliver a strong sense of order and take personal responsibility for action and for keeping things in proper sequence and use.*

Core Alignment Meditation

Part 1 *Right hand over left, palms face down at heart level. Thumb tips touch and point toward chest. Chant the sound* **Har** *(the creative energy of Infinity or God) at a steady pace. With each* **Har** *pull in the navel point and lift the chest up and forward. Then release the navel and allow your lower spine to rock back slightly.*

Continue for 3 to 11 minutes.

Part 2 *Put hands in prayer pose with the thumbs crossed. Inhale deeply and begin to "chop" with the hands as you chant* **Har.**
Do it steadily 12X as your turn left, then 12X back to center, then 12X turning to the right, and finally 12X back to center. Inhale deeply; begin again.

Continue for 11 to 31 minutes. To end, inhale and hold the breath, press the molars together, and continue the motion for one full cycle. Relax. This meditation will integrate your time and how your internal self deals with all the projections through time.

"Relay of a Past Memory"

Negative Mind x Ahangkar/Negative

Memories flow constantly into our awareness. The Negative Mind sorts these to use only the ones that support your action and identity. **Too strong,** *and you can become fearful of past mistakes and traumas. You may be slow to change and need high levels of confidence before committing to a direction of action. You require evidence and repetition of things already certain.* **Too weak,** *and you are blind-sided by things you could have avoided through using past lessons. You let angers and frustrations from the past submerge and develop subconsciously.* **Balanced,** *you learn quickly from the past, avoid your own traumas and those of others, and can rapidly come up with new plans to avoid old errors and clean up past messes. You will be highly ethical and feel best when you can forgive all the errors you find others have made, as you create new ways to move ahead.*

Synchronization Meditation

Cross-heart Kirtan Kriya

Sit straight. Cross the forearms, below the wrists, and hold them in front of the chest. Arms out slightly, palms up and a little toward the chest. Look down the tip of the nose. Begin to chant:

Saa taa naa maa

—as you play the fingers by touching the thumb tip to the fingertip of the index, then middle, then ring, then little finger.

Continue 11 to 31 minutes.

Then inhale, hold, roll the eyes up, and become completely still. Relax.

The hemispheres will balance; the past will be processed and dumped; and insecurity will vaporize.

"Phase of a Mental Projection"
Negative Mind x Ahangkar/Positve

*You have projected and attracted your relations, associates, and resources at some point in time. Now act on and utilize those resources as responses to your purpose. **Too much**, and you manipulate and become what others need rather than what you are. **Too little**, and you absorb into others with loss of self. **Balanced**, and you are flexible, socially facile, secure, and able to handle the expectations of group and role.*

Synchronization Meditation

Part 1 *Sit straight. Elbows by the sides. Hands are at heart level and separated the width of the chest. Put the palms facing up as if to catch water. Eyes are 1/10th open. Regulate the breath: inhale 20 seconds, hold 20 seconds, and exhale slowly for 20 seconds.*

Continue 11 to 31 minutes.

Part 2 *While maintaining the same position, immediately begin to chant **Har** at a steady pace. With each **Har** pull in the navel point and pull the fingers into the palm, like calling someone towards you.*

Continue for 3 minutes.

Then inhale deeply, make tight fists. Relax.

"Shadow of a Mental Projection"

Negative Mind x Ahangkar/Neutral

Every cause has an impact and an orbit of effect. This Projection uses the Neutral Mind to intuit all the expected and unexpected impacts of the mental thoughts you feel now or that in the past were a part of you. **Too much,** *and people become socially distant out of subconscious fear of your perception, bluntness, and truth.* **Too little,** *sells short the benefits and grace of the universe from your actions. Accidents happen.* **Balanced,** *you gain wisdom and self-guidance to hold in trust all that comes to you. You are never swayed by abundance and hold closely to the path.*

Synchronization Meditation

Sit with a straight spine. Put elbows by the sides; forearms parallel to the ground, pointing forward; palms face up; wrists straight. Touch the thumb tips to the tips of the index fingers. Look down the tip of the nose. Chant in a steady cadence:

Har ha-ray ha-ree
Wha-hay gu-roo

Three qualities of **Har:**
seed, flow, and completion.
Ecstatic Infinity of God

Continue for 11 to 31 minutes.

This meditation provides guidance and the way through any block is yours. The future is clear, without anxiety.

Negative Mind x Buddhi

Qualities: In the midst of all thoughts, emotions, and commotion, this Aspect keeps you on the path. **Too strong**, you can be a nag and a wise-guy always full of advice to correct the errors of other people. Focused through your self, you can become fixed on a solution that is not on the surface, sometimes far-fetched imaginings or ideologies, that put you into an observant, safe, and judgmentally powerful position. **Too weak**, and you act too slowly to threats, especially ones that are evidenced by strong emotions or by future rather than immediate impacts. Instead of preserving you only salvage. When **balanced**, you can say, and mean, "All this life is Your gift. The pain and tragedy is as sweet as nectar." You are alert to any positive or negative impact that can sway you from your essential path. You can find the silver lining in any cloud. You defend by awareness, not by reaction or threat. You guide your project between all the interests that would interfere or stop it. You pass the challenges and sail toward fulfillment.

Core Alignment Meditation

Sit straight. Place the right palm on the back of the left hand. Both palms face down in front of your torso at the level of the heart center. Eyes are at the tip of the nose or 1/10th open. Chant the following 3 times on a single breath.

Ha-ree naam sat naam ha-ree naam ha-ree
Ha-ree naam sat naam sat naam ha-ree

Continue for 31 minutes.

It is a mantra and meditation that keeps you on the path. This meditation will integrate your time and how your internal self deals with all the projections through time.

"Deep Memory of a Past Projection"
Negative Mind x Buddhi/Negative

Past Projections can tempt, hypnotize, and distract us. A deep memory holds the impact of trauma, of disruptions of our identity. This Projection goes away from that. It is cautious about intensity from the past. **Too much** of this Projection, and depression, detachment, and lower learning develop. **Too little**, and nostalgia, procrastination, and regrets dominate. When **balanced**, you become a rapid social learner. You are quick to avoid past temptations, and are able to let go of things that do not concern or serve you now.

Synchronization Meditation

Sit straight. Eyes look at the tip of the nose. Place the fingertips of each hand together with the other hand. Form a "teepee," and place it in front of the torso at the level of the solar plexus. Fingers are spread and facing forward. Inhale deeply through the nose. Hold as you mentally chant **Saa taa naa maa** once. Then exhale by segmenting the breath in eight equal strokes. Breathe out through the rounded mouth. The exhale is not from the tip of the lips; it comes from the middle of the mouth and is generated from the navel. By the eighth exhale, pull the navel point all the way back towards the spine.

Continue for 11 minutes. Increase the time slowly to 31 minutes.

The past is dropped. The five elements clear to reveal your real self. You see all without being caught. Let go, let flow.

"Mental Intersection"
Negative Mind x Buddhi/Positive

*This Projection is resourceful, inventive, and expansive. You gain clarity and insights into self and circumstance and find the ability to make useful connections. **Too much** of this Projection, and you will feel prematurely complete, jump the gun on action without full depth. **Too little**, and you will feel somewhat dependent on others and the environment around you. **Balanced**, you feel complete. Resources appear all around you. You can accurately assess your current skill, impact, and the connections created from your efforts.*

Synchronization Meditation

Sit straight with elbows by your sides. Place your hands at shoulder height by your sides, with palms forward and hands in Gian Mudra (index finger tip on the thumb tip). Pull the shoulders back and lock them. Look at the tip of the nose. Chant in a steady, clipped or marching cadence:

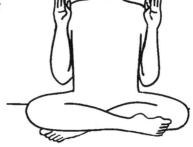

Har har wha-hay gu-roo

*Use one complete breath for each repetition of the mantra. Use the tip of the tongue on **Har**, and move the lips distinctly on the rest.*

Continue for 31 minutes.

As the sound walks up your spine, you balance all the five elements and passions in the midst of activity.

"Mental Outer Projection"

Negative Mind x Buddhi/Neutral

*The neutral and buddhi parts of the mind dominate in this Projection. The result is a clear perception of what is important to preserve. You perceive that it is connected with the wider flow of the universe, both known and Unknown. This Projection links the essence of your purpose to the greater minds and souls in the cosmos. Your message and need are projected into them, and help and knowledge come back to serve you and complete your goal. It is a prayerful Projection for a unified response from the universe. **Too much** of this projection, and you miss the cues for action that complete the cycle of projection to the greater mind and back to you. **Too little**, and you can feel isolated and detached. **Balanced**, you rely on the heavens and greater environment. You feel a conversation with the universe. Synchronicity is common. "At the last minute, the Grace of the Guru saves the disciple."*

Synchronization Meditation

Sit with a straight spine. Hold the hands at the level of the heart center. The right hand is on back of the left hand, both palms face down. The right thumb is bent and comes under the left hand and touches the palm. The left thumb is bent and also touches the left palm. The bent thumbs are pressed together so the thumbnails touch. Look at the tip of the nose.

Chant the following mantra:

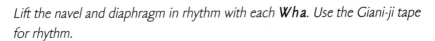

Wha-hay gu-roo wha-hay gu-roo wha-hay gu-roo wha-hay jeeo

*Lift the navel and diaphragm in rhythm with each **Wha**. Use the Giani-ji tape for rhythm.*

Continue for 31 minutes.

Positive Mind x Manas

Qualities: *This Aspect gives you extraordinary sensitivity to sensations, emotions, and impressions from nature and other people. Its basic urge is to create, elaborate, and express each sensation.* **Too strong,** *you seem bewitched by special people, places, and things. You see a richness that pulls you powerfully towards a sensation. You take risks, flirt with addictions, and find only positive impacts in tragedy, intense experiences, and change. You underestimate the future impact of your present actions and explorations.* **Too weak,** *you lack spontaneous joy from all that happens and retreat to internal imagination to feel good. You suspect the passion you see in others has some other motive than stimulation or pleasure. You try to moderate your own desire to safe levels.* **Balanced,** *the Artist explores every feeling by creating something to experience, to amplify, or to repeat. It is concerned with proportions, blends, and how to utilize what it senses. It is open to all opinions and loves diversity. Curiosity, wonder, and impatience are frequent moods for this Aspect. Your life becomes a work of art or an idiosyncratic piece of work. Moderation and dedication are essential.*

Core Alignment Meditation

Sit straight. Spread the fingers of each hand wide with the palms facing up. Touch the sides of the tips of the sun (ring) fingers together. The hands will slightly overlap with the left little finger lower than the right. No fingers other than the sun fingers should be touching. Place the mudra at the level of the heart center. Eyes look down toward fingers. Mentally chant **Saa taa naa maa** *as in Kirtan Kriya, as you mentally pulse the thumb tip with each fingertip in sequence. Breathe slow and deep, four times a minute or less.*

Continue for 31 minutes.

"The Art of Memorizing Creativity"
Positive Mind x Manas/Negative

This Projection explores sensations with a need for security or confirmation. It is receptive, enthusiastic, and appreciative. It seeks certainty and stimulation by repetition. It is sensitive to past imprints from deep emotions, exceptional events, and strong personalities. If **too strong**, there is a tendency to idealize heroes, teachers, and leaders. You confirm your value by what you find in others and what you can recognize and imitate. If it is **too weak**, you will be self-conscious and too critical. You will be reserved and full of feelings you assume others can see. **Balanced** it helps you to feel secure, and you immerse yourself into an experience or role without losing a confirmed sense of your self and your own contribution. You can present, perform, and advocate things you discover in the world to enhance both creativity and your self.

Synchronization Meditation

Karani Kriya

Sit with straight spine. Raise the arms in front of the torso with the forearms parallel to the ground at shoulder height. Bend the elbows so the fingers can point toward each other in front of the throat center, palms facing down. Bend the ring and little fingers under the thumb on the palm. Extend and touch the tips of the index and middle fingers to the tips of the opposite hand. Close the eyes to 1/10th open. Create a precisely timed pattern of pranayama:

Inhale for 2 to 3 seconds. Hold the breath in for 5 seconds. Completely exhale for 10 to 15 seconds.

Continue for 11 to 31 minutes. Then inhale deeply. Relax.

This kriya will help the aspirant find the source of creativity that is in the heart. It solves the problem of finding how to make a lucrative livelihood and satisfy the soul at the same time.

"The Art of Creating Art"

Positive Mind x Manas/Positive

This Projection is up-beat, positive, and loaded with high expectations. It is oriented towards a goal. It loves the feeling of action and completion more than the thing produced. If it is **too strong**, you will be a workaholic. Things you have attained and your personal image are important measures of your self-worth. If it is **too weak**, you either lose your focus and fail to complete your project, or you are driven to complete it but don't know what step to take. When **balanced** you instinctively organize sequences of production details and are masterful at guiding projects to completion.

Synchronization Meditation

Tapa Yog Karam Kriya

Sit in a meditative pose. The arms are straight and extended forward parallel to the ground. Palms face each other. Put the wrists together. Then spread the palms apart as far as you can as though pushing against a wall. The eyes are slightly open looking down at the tip of the nose. Begin to rhythmically chant:

**Sat naam sat naam sat naam
Sat naam sat naam sat naam
Wha-hay gu-roo**

Continue for 11 minutes.

This kriya develops will power and gives the capacity to understand the elements of your personality. It is perfect to overcome difficulty in completing projects and doing what you intend.

"The Art of Creating Creativity"

Positive Mind x Manas/Neutral

Besides the enthusiasm to create something from what is sensed, this projection goes beyond the surface. The result is not just art, but art that has originality. It is creativity infused with an inner cohesion that comes from a vision of the uniqueness that exists in this moment of time and in these particular sensations. **Too much**, and you can struggle unnecessarily with deeper meanings and a feeling of emptiness. **Too little**, and you can overestimate your efforts and settle for average rather than putting in the continued effort for excellence. When **balanced** this Projection has a perspective and detachment from its own desires. It is able to add a guiding style, signature, or aesthetic that elevates passion to purpose, and fancy to enchantment.

Synchronization Meditation

Sit straight. Place both hands in front of the torso, just above the solar plexus and at the base of the heart center. Both palms are face up. Right hand rests in the left. Forearms are parallel to the ground. Extend both thumbs stiffly pointing straightforward away form the chest. Eyes are 1/10th open looking down the nose. Inhale very deeply and on a single breath chant:

Ha-ree ha-ree ha-ree ha-ree
Ha-ree ha-ree haaaar

A monotone is fine. The last sound of **Har** is extended as if you project the sound gradually to the Infinite. You can imagine a beautiful spring-green color expanding from every pore of your body to the cosmos with the last sound.

Continue 11 to 31 minutes.

ASPECT 5 • PRODUCER

Positive Mind x Ahangkar

Qualities: *The Positive Mind is about creating and utilizing. Ahangkar establishes our boundaries and domain through attachments and passions. The combination is an Aspect that seeks and gives the ability to enhance, extend, and utilize anything that enters your sense of domain. You attach more to the fact of doing, to completion of a creation, than to the specific creation itself. You are inspired by the bliss of intending an action and having it happen. The joy of intelligent effective action is all around you. If it is* **too strong***, you can leap before you check the downsides. You assume if it comes into your domain, you should do something with it. It is hard to let go of things even if they are not your task. "I am worthy if I work" is a common theme. If this Aspect is* **too weak***, you have many ideas but lack a practical sense of how to do it, or you feel insecure about whether it can really happen. The insecurity is "Will I succeed?" When* **balanced** *you put things in to sequences that lead to desired consequences. You organize resources in your self and others to deliver a project, goal, and creation. You can be very serious and focused. You quickly discern what is your task and what is not. You are often loyal and effective in a well-defined role.*

Core Alignment Meditation

Sit in a meditative pose with spine erect. Arms by the sides with elbows bent to 90 degrees and palms facing each other at the level of the navel. Eyes are 1/10ᵗʰ open or looking down the nose. Chant the mantra:

Har har har har gobinday	*God God God God Sustainer*
Har har har har mukanday	*God God God God Liberator*
Har har har har udaaray	*God God God God Uplifter*
Har har har har apaaray	*God God God God Carrying Through*
Har har har har hareeang	*God God God God Destroyer of All*
Har har har har kareeang	*God God God God Creator of All*
Har har har har nirnaamay	*God God God God Beyond Category*
Har har har har akaamay	*God God God God Beyond Desire*

With each chant of the sound **Har** *pulse the hands in toward each other then back out. The movement is about 6 inches. It is quick, forceful, and precise. Hold the hands still for the other sounds such as* **Gobinday.**

Continue for 31 minutes. To end, inhale deeply, tighten the forearms, hands, and fingers. Focus at the brow. Exhale powerfully through the mouth. Do this three times. Relax.

"Creating Art Through Past Memory"

Positive Mind x Ahangkar/Negative

*When **balanced**, this Projection acts like a gourmet that intensifies sensations and experiences them very personally. There is a tendency to be a collector, to acquire things that will express your feelings and ideals. The positive feelings of the past are savored, repeated, and refined. It becomes a way to feel who you are. It is an aesthetic of the personal past. At best this can lead to a storyteller, one who unites a family and relationships from a sense of history and ancestors. If it is **too strong**, the attachment tendency of ahangkar can dominate. Then it devolves into a cloying nostalgia or an attachment to miseries of the past as a way to belong. The writer Salinger did not publish a story for decades after "Catcher in the Rye." He said it was to keep the experiences he wrote about as his own, undisturbed by the thoughts and feelings of others. When it is **too weak**, you can lack the ability to set boundaries on the intense feelings of the past—you become entangled with them, without distinguishing the positive and negative impacts of the past feelings. Or, with less ahangkar, you cannot rank your own experiences easily to set priorities. All of your experiences seem distanced or emotionally flat. You are a gourmet without strong opinions and with a blunted palate.*

Synchronization Meditation

Heart Shield Meditation

Sit straight, with the left hand in front of the heart center, palm facing the chest 4 to 6 inches away. Keep the fingers stiff but not tight. The forearm is parallel to the ground. The right arm is straight, resting over the knee. Hold the right hand in Gian Mudra, with the forefinger curled under the thumb and the other fingers straight and joined. Eyes look down the nose. Chant:

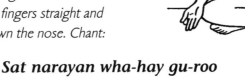

Sat narayan wha-hay gu-roo
Ha-ree narayan sat naam

True Sustainer Indescribable Wisdom
Creative Sustainer True Identity

Continue for 11 minutes. Then inhale, hold briefly and relax. Meditate with open awareness as your heart center adjusts your feelings with the boundaries of the self.

"Creating Art by Environmental Effects"
Positive Mind x Ahangkar/Positive

*This Projection is a power of the builder. It combines a sensation-seeker with a pragmatic creative streak that asks, "How can I do something with this?" Everything that is seen is considered a potential for "my purpose." You have seen artists wrap entire islands in pink plastic, and make a pattern of lights across continents to be seen by passing satellites. Research scientists who are building tools from individual atoms are using this Projection when it comes to creating the engineering vision. If this Projection is **too strong** you can be insensitive to the impact on others and on the environments you interact with. **Too weak** and you have new theories and perceptions, but not the risk-taking attitude needed to initiate them. When **balanced** there is no hesitation to see the potential of the environment in terms of how it is useful for your project.*

Synchronization Meditation

Sit straight. Palms together in prayer pose at the heart center. Focus at the brow point. Inhale deeply and chant on a single breath:

Raa raa raa raa
Maa maa maa maa
Raamaa raamaa raamaa raamaa
Saa taa naa maa

(**Raa** *is the sun energy,* **Maa** *is the moon energy*)

Continue for 11 to 31 minutes.

Then inhale, hold the breath and press palms together strongly. Exhale. Repeat three times and relax.

This meditation will keep the balance of boundaries and focus as resources and recognition pour in. It keeps you centered under the polarities and vectors of contention that come with any significant project in life. It also increases creativity of the archetypal masculine/feminine mix.

"Creating Art by Projecting into the Future"

Positive Mind x Ahangkar/Neutral

The future, the vision of what each seed will become, is tangible. This Projection gives you confidence in your assessment of the reality of your own efforts. You are an alchemist of the future self. "How can I leverage what I have by astute assessment of what is and see what becomes?" In business you are an entrepreneur, in art a visionary, in science a researcher, in religion a revitalizing reformer. When **balanced** *you display a combination of gut instincts, cool assessment, and strong personal ownership of the action.* **Too much,** *and you can stand alone in your vision. You may become embittered or cynical at the lack of clarity in others to comprehend what you know as a fact.* **Too little**, *and you sense the right direction to go but seek more confirmation from others. You might also test others for their loyalty to your ideas, to be sure of your own vision.*

Synchronization Meditation

Naad Meditation: to Communicate from Totality

Part 1 *Sit straight in easy pose. Close the eyes or keep them 1/10th open. Bring the hands next to the shoulders with the palms forward, the fingers pointing up, and the wrists straight. Relax the elbows by your sides. Place each hand in Gian Mudra. Inhale and chant the following mantra in a strong monotone cadence:*

Wha wha hay hay, Wha wha hay hay
Wha wha hay hay, Gu-roo

With each sound, move both hands forward and back quickly as if you were throwing darts. They should move forward 12 to 18 inches. Inhale after **Guroo** *while the hands pause. Continue for 11 to 31 minutes.*

Part 2 *Immediately sit straight and place the hands on top of the head. Interlace the fingers. Create a mild pressure on top of the head. Twist smoothly side to side. Inhale as you twist left, exhale right. Continue for 3 minutes. Inhale to the center and hold the breath as you concentrate on the crown of the head. Then relax.*

This meditation lets you merge into the feeling of totality. When you speak from that feeling you create trust. With trust you establish strong relationships.

Positive Mind x Buddhi

Qualities: *The Positive Mind gives the quality of action, involvement, and passion. It gives the power to grasp and magnify. The Buddhi Mind gives discernment about what is real and from your own essence. It also gives you intuition to see through time and to discern the cycle of time. The result is to pursue the expression of an essence through time.* **Too strong**, *and you leap into good work or push a good thing at the wrong place or time. You project your essence or destiny onto others and assume they are ready and want what you have seen. You become preachy and pushy. Impatience leads to poor judgement. This is the downfall of many spiritual leaders.* **Too weak**, *you could leap towards temporary success in the spirit of the cause. You do not accept feedback from others, nor see the full impact of your actions since you are convinced they are positive. You pursue success rather than the cycle of success. When this Aspect is* **balanced** *you are successful and strategic in action, not just tactical. You have an expanded sense of life. You feel that the Infinite Will and yours act together. Strong actions combined with non-attachment make life a dance with much creativity and gratitude.*

Core Alignment Meditation

Kundalini Yoga Laya Meditation

Sit straight. Put the palms together in prayer pose at the center of the chest. Focus through the brow point. Chant:

Ek ong kaar-a, Saa taa naa maa-a, Siree whaa-a, Hay gu-roo
One Creator Creation   True Identity   Great Indescribable Wisdom

The chant is very precise. On **Ek** *pull in the navel. On each "a" lift the diaphragm up firmly. Relax the navel and abdomen on* **Hay guroo**. *The sound has a "spin" to it. It is a 3 -1/2 cycle rhythm. As you chant, imagine energy and sound spiraling up and around the spinal cord in a right-handed helix. Start at the base of the spine as you initiate the energy form the navel. End with focus over the head to the Cosmos on* **Hay guroo**.

Continue for 31 minutes. This extraordinary Laya Yoga Chant will bring your soul and destiny present. It will suspend you above conflicts attracted by success and the activity of the Positive Mind. It will let your activity serve your purpose. It will make you creative and focused on your real priorities, and help you sacrifice what is needed to accomplish them.

"Pursuing the Cycle of Success"
Positive Mind x Buddhi/Negative

This Projection recognizes the cycles of acceptance and rejection and holds through the ups and downs devoted to the end. If **too strong**, you tend to blame and project on others, an inquisition, to assure the protection of what you know to be true. If it is **weak**, you may become judgemental, reclusive, or bitter. **Balanced**, it gives the capacity to find supporters in your skeptics and opponents. It holds you steady through upsets and makes you non-reactive. You attract through the greater mind.

Synchronization Meditation

Chakra Balance Meditation

Sit straight in easy pose. Relax the arms down along the sides. Draw the hands together at the level of the diaphragm. Point the left palm toward the body. Then make a fist of the left hand with the thumb inside. Enclose this fist with the right hand, closing the right thumb over top. Press the elbow firmly against the sides of the chest. Fix the eyes 1/10th open, looking down at the tip of the nose. Chant steadily:

Ha-ree har   Ha-ree har
Ha-ree har   Ha-ree har
Ha-ree har   Ha-ree har
Ha-ree har   Ha-ree har

As you chant each of the 8 repetitions, gently pulse the navel point. Mentally walk the sounds up the 7 chakras from the base up to the crown and out to the surrounding auric light for the 8th repetition.

Continue for 11 to 31 minutes. Then inhale deeply, relax, and dwell in your vastness, contentment, and balance with the cycles of life. This meditation balances the chakras so you may explore the inner realms of infinity.

"Pursuing the Cycle of Artistic Attributes"
Positive Mind x Buddhi/Positive

*When you see the reality of something, you know the impact it can have. You want to share it, extend it, and promote it. This Projection seeks balance and proportion. It wants to express its insight without distorting the core. If this is **too weak**, you are satisfied with imagination or with the sensation of pleasure from knowing you could do something. It is like cooking without eating the food. If this is **too strong**, you eat the food but it is half-baked. You are subject to emotional and spiritual fads. Your caliber will be limited due to magnification and distortion. In **balance**, people and the cosmos feel your dedication like a burning flame. Your enthusiasm inflames and enlists the resources needed to reach your goal.*

Synchronization Meditation

Sit straight. Put both hands palms up in front of your torso. Elbows close to the sides. Chant steadily as you pull in the navel point:

Har har har har har...

*The chant is continuous and regular. The pace is the same as the tape "Tantric Har." As you chant each **Har**, trace outward circles with both hands, keeping the palms up. The circles are about 12 inches in diameter. As the arms come back along the sides, the elbows hit the sides of the torso definitively. Coordinate the sounding of the mantra, the pulling of the navel, and circling of the hands until they are a single flow.*

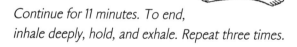

Continue for 11 minutes. To end, inhale deeply, hold, and exhale. Repeat three times.

"Pursuing the Art of Cohesiveness"

Positive Mind x Buddhi/Neutral

*The mind is cohesive when all the thoughts flow around a central focus. When it establishes a consolidated attitude it guides all of the senses to enrich and elaborate that central focus. When **balanced**, this Projection uses that laser-like focus to plant seeds, core concepts, and feelings. The Projection can hold the mind's attention to that seed thought so that it is nurtured by all the other activities in the mind, and it eventually unfolds and bears fruit. This Projection also gives you the insight to recognize the quality of uniqueness in your words and actions. You feel like a creator who acts and finds the reflections of that act everywhere. **Too weak**, and you are unclear what seed you planted. You mistake one thought for another. **Too strong**, and you become detached instead of staying active to insure the seed develops. You lose the sense of ownership over your creations.*

Synchronization Meditation

Part 1 *Sit straight with the right hand in a pledge position near the shoulder, palm forward, fingers up, wrist straight, elbow by the side. The left hand is palm up, as if to catch water, elbow by the side, hand at heart level slightly in front of the torso. Look down the nose. Inhale steadily and deeply through the rounded lips. Exhale slowly through the nose. Keep the breath powerful and less than four times a minute. Continue 11 to 31 minutes.*

Part 2 *Immediately cross the hands over the heart center, right over left. Close the eyes. Have the thought of STILLNESS or no thought. Let everything go through you without reaction. Breathe extremely slowly and meditatively. Continue for 3 minutes.*

Part 3 *Without a break put both palms flat together in prayer pose. Place the middle joints of the thumbs on the brow point. Focus at the brow and chant:*

Ong namo gu-roo dev namo

I bow to the Creator, I bow to the Divine Wisdom

Feel the vibration at the brow point and in the entire skull.

Continue for 3 to 11 minutes. Inhale deeply, press the palms together as you squeeze the spine, roll the eyes up and concentrate your energy at the brow. Exhale forcefully through the mouth. Repeat this breath three times. Relax.

Neutral Mind x Manas

Qualities: *The Neutral Mind gives you a constant assessment of and alertness to whatever comes to you. Manas makes you aware of impressions made in your senses, in your environment itself, or through subconscious imprints. You are less aware of your self as a subject. You seek a perspective on things and events that lets you sense the reality and long-term impact of your actions.* **Too strong,** *you are cool, collected, and not involved. You decide about actions and things very accurately but miss the impact on your personal life and relationships. You can also be a dedicated to finding an answer in the material, the seen, and the provable.* **Too weak,** *you will be entangled in the results and impacts on people of your actions. You may have conflicts over: duty versus love, effort versus reward, or roles versus your own sense of authenticity.* **Balanced,** *you find meanings and consequences in events that others do not. Your agenda is impersonally personal. You don't mind losing a battle if you win the war. Small clues reveal pathways others have simply overlooked. You can find and arrange resources masterfully. You may not manage them operationally, but you can recognize, attract, and gather them.*

Core Alignment Meditation

Sit straight. Start by interlacing the fingers, one hand into the other. Now, extend the little fingers, ring fingers, and middle fingers so they lay against the same fingers of the opposite hand, and so all point straight up. Separate the base of the palms about 4 inches so the three fingers form a teepee, and a round space opens between the two index fingers, on top, and the two thumbs, below. Raise this mudra up to your face and put your nose in the opening between index fingers and thumbs. The index fingers rest near the bridge of the nose. The thumbs cross just under the nose but do not block the nostrils. The other fingers point straight up. Elbows are relaxed. Focus at the brow point and chant the following mantra.

Har har gobinday	*Sustains You*
Har har mukanday	*Liberates You*
Har har udaaray	*Elevates You*
Har har apaaray	*Delivers You Across*
Har har hareeang	*Destroys All*
Har har kareeang	*Creates All*
Har har nirnaamay	*Beyond Category & Name*
Har har akaamay	*Beyond Desire*

Each line of the mantra has two **Hars** *and another word to make three beats. As you chant press the tips of the three fingers in sequence. Begin with the middle fingertips pressing firmly on the first* **Har**. *Then the ring fingers on the next* **Har**, *and finally the little fingertips on Gobinday. For the next line begin* **Har** *on the little fingertips and work forward. Continue through all 8 lines of the mantra, so you end back on the middle finger tips. As you chant these motions become smooth and automatic. Then your attention goes deep into the sound itself. Continue for 11 to 31 minutes. Then inhale deeply, hold, and focus at the brow. Then exhale powerfully through the mouth. Repeat this final breath sequence three times, and then relax.*

PROJECTION 19 • SCOUT

"Judging Environments Through the Senses"
Neutral Mind x Manas/Negative

*When **balanced**, this Projection assesses the environment knowing that there may be dangers. It finds the edge that gives you hair-trigger efficiency and an advantage in a situation. It helps you to have steadiness and strong nerves under stress. If it is **too strong**, you search but do not find; you date but do not commit; you feel the answer is out there, just one more hill away. If it is **too weak**, you can become absorbed or entranced by some part of the environment and forget your own agendas.*

Synchronization Meditation

Sit with spine erect. Raise the hands up in front of the chest at heart center level, palms facing the torso and fingers parallel to the ground. Place the palm of the right hand on the back of the left hand. Join the thumb tips and point them up. Balance the arms so the shoulders are relaxed and the forearms parallel to the ground. Keep the eyes 1/10th open. Inhale deeply through the nose and hold for 10 seconds. Then exhale completely as you pull in the navel center and hold the breath out for 10 seconds.

Continue this breathing pattern for 11 minutes. (You can also practice it for just 3 to 5 minutes to quickly switch on this capacity.)

"Judging Environments"
Neutral Mind x Manas/Positive

*There are many resources within you and in your environment. This Projection allows you to select them according to your goals. When **balanced** you see things for what they really are. You know what they can provide and how they will help your project. You have a sense of limits but also a sense of how to sequence the approach to be practical. Ultimately you find a way through. **Too much** of this Projection and you rely on yourself too much. You do not manage your resources well since you are sure everyone has the same dedication to the goal and will stay the course. **Too little**, and you will miss opportunities that are right before you. You will hesitate when it is time to act, or not express enough passion for the goal since you assume it is right and should just happen.*

Synchronization Meditation

Sit straight. Extend both arms forward and up until the fingertips are just above the level of the top of your head. Elbows and wrists are straight. The palms face down and the thumbs interlock, one over the other. Keep the rest of the fingers straight and do not touch fingers of the opposite hands. Close the eyes. Inhale deeply and chant this mantra four times on one breath as you exhale:

Sat naam sat naam sat naam
Sat naam sat naam sat naam
Wha-hay gu-roo

Continue for 11 minutes. Gradually you can increase this to 31 minutes. It is excellent at any age and especially beneficial if practiced when young, at about seven years old. It will enhance intelligence and competence to assess the environments and perform to maximum capacity.

"Judging Positive Environments Through Intuition"
Neutral Mind x Manas/Neutral

*This Projection sees below the surface and knows with intuition the connections and consequences associated with a situation. When **balanced** it guides you to actions that are conscious and graceful. It knows which way to step, who to associate with, and how to maintain your identity in any environment. If it is **too strong**, you will be attached to the insights you find everywhere. You may have a tendency to act like a psychic or master the environments through advice instead of action. If it is **too weak**, you will react to the environments and find yourself drawn away from your main path. You will think strategy is the same as opportunism and confuse flexibility with lack of direction from your own inner compass.*

Synchronization Meditation

Kirtan Kriya

Sit straight in easy pose. Meditate at the brow point and chant the mantra:

Saa taa naa maa

*Each repetition of the mantra takes 3-4 seconds. While chanting the elbows are straight and each fingertip touches in turn the tip of the thumb with firm pressure. On **Saa** touch the index finger to the thumb. On **Taa** touch the middle finger to the thumb. On **Naa** touch the ring finger to the thumb. On **Maa** touch the little finger to the thumb. Then begin again at the index finger. Chant in the three languages of consciousness: human (normal or loud voice), lovers (whispered), and divine (silent). Begin the kriya in a normal voice for 5 minutes, then whisper for 5 minutes and then go deep into the sound and vibrate it silently for 10 minutes. Then come back to a whisper for 5 minutes, and end with a normal voice for 5 minutes.*

*Saa is Infinity. **Taa** is Life. **Naa** is Death. **Maa** is Rebirth/Transformation. This describes the cycle of life. This kriya brings a total mental balance to the psyche.*

Neutral Mind x Ahangkar

Qualities: *This Aspect combines the qualities of critical assessment with that of owner-ship or responsibility for action. It is developed and* **balanced** *in great leaders. A leader must look ahead and beyond the surface. There is a mental habit to constantly assess everything even in the midst of great absorption to the task at hand. The combination lets you hold each boundary and division of role with integrity and accuracy. It gives you the capacity for superior manners and social interaction. The Neutral Mind helps you evaluate each person and each resource or prize that comes to you for what it can and cannot do. The ability to see beyond the surface lets you call on the talent and hidden potential of each person. That builds trust and loyalty when used with respect for each person and with the focus that moves everyone to reach a goal.* **Too strong**, *and you can become reactive or emotional when people seem to forget your goals and direction. Passion applied in the right place is inspiration, but passion reacting without a sense of place or timing is not good leadership even if it stirs people.* **Too weak**, *you confuse your own agenda with that of your task or duty. As a leader, you shift the goal and mis-takenly identify who is for your interests and who is against them.*

Core Alignment Meditation

Sit on your heels with a straight spine. Stretch the arms straight out in front, parallel to the ground. The palms are flat and facing the ground; the fingers point straight forward. The arms will be shoulder-width apart. As you chant the mantra you will alternately raise the arms up to 60 degrees and then return them to their original position as follows:

Aadays	*raise arms up to 60 degrees*
Tisai	*arms straight out in front of you*
Aadays	*up to 60 degrees*
Aad	*straight in front*
Aneel	*up to 60 degrees*
Anaad	*straight in front*
Anaahat	*up to 60 degrees*
Jug-jug	*straight in front*
Ayko	*up to 60 degrees*
Vays	*straight in front*

Keep the hands and elbows held straight out firmly, with no bends. Chin is pulled in slightly.

The mantra is spoken in a continuous monotone, in a precise beat with a projection of strength. Each word is spoken individually, with a slight pause between each word, except **Jug-jug***, which is run together as one word. Speak from the navel point. This meditation rids you of fears and split personalities. Continue for 31 minutes. To end, inhale deeply. Relax.*

"Assessment of the Position"

Neutral Mind x Ahangkar/Negative

This Projection is always crystal clear about the territory, task, and people it is responsible for. When **balanced** you instantly understand your role, the resources available, and the job you can do. This Projection is more concerned to not lose, to defend, and to hold on to what has been gained. It is an excellent source of feedback about the weakness in your position and personality. **Too strong** and you will underestimate the sacrifices you and others must make to accomplish something. **Too weak** and you will have a tendency toward naiveté. You may lead down primrose paths that go over cliffs, or be envious of the positions of others.

Synchronization Meditation

Haumei Bandana Kriya

Sit in easy pose with a straight spine. Relax the arms down with the elbows bent. Make fists of the hands with the thumbs extended out from the fists. Raise the forearms up and in toward each other until the thumbs touch each other. No fingers of the opposite hands touch each other at any time. Apply 25 pounds of pressure per square inch on the thumbs. Hold the hand position in front of the chest at the heart level. Deeply inhale and chant the mantra:

Wha-hay wha-hay wha-hay gu-roo

four times in a monotone voice as the breath is exhaled completely. It may be increased to 8 repetitions per breath.

Continue for a maximum of 31 minutes.

This meditation takes away your self-pride and vanity.

"Assessment of the Successful"
Neutral Mind x Ahangkar/Positive

Two characteristics of this Projection stand out: it is optimistic and active in moving itself and others toward its goal; and it is confident and needs no other justification. When **balanced** it establishes a clear evaluation of what it acquires as it succeeds, so short-term gains are assessed in terms of long-term values. It is not enough to win or to own something; it must also serve your goal. Otherwise it is a distraction. This lucidity gives you a natural magnetizing quality that directs and commands others to accomplish your priorities and projects. **Too much**, and you can appear emotionally cool and have an air of personal entitlement. **Too little**, and you will accept resources, gifts, and successes but stop or pause in motivation, thus denying the larger goal because things seem okay already.

Synchronization Meditation

Sit in easy pose with a straight spine. Relax the arms down with the elbows bent. Raise the hands to shoulder level with the palms facing forward. The hands, elbows, and shoulders are in the same plane. The shoulder blades join in equal parallel lines. The first two and last two fingers are touching and you spread the fingers between the second and third fingers (like Spock's greeting). The thumbs are stretched away from the hands. Very gracefully inhale in 10 equal parts and exhale in 10 equal parts. Hold the breath after each inhale and exhale and mentally chant with the breath held:

Aad sach	True in the beginning
Jugaad sach	True throughout the ages
Haibhee sach	True even now
Naanak hosee bhee sach	Nanak says Truth shall ever be

Continue for 11 to 31 minutes. After finishing, inhale and exhale deeply 3 times.

This meditation will carry you through a confined situation to a very unconfined situation, so that you may know that beyond your world there is another world, so you may start searching for that world.

"Assessment of Personality & Facets Through Intuition"

Neutral Mind x Ahangkar/Neutral

*This Projection supports you to act on your duty and to deliver your identity regardless of conditions. It builds your projection of character. When refined and **balanced**, your deep insight into situations and people lets you instinctively know what someone will really do for your project and what they won't. You can utilize people in ways that bring success to them and to you. You inspire confidence and people follow you automatically based on your judgement. It gives you the capacity to apply a regime of change and development within yourself. You never are depressed by blockages. Your rule is that there is no such thing as failure only feedback, lessons, and new strategies. You can demand and evoke the best from your staff and team. If it is **too strong**, you may assume everyone knows himself or herself as clearly as you do. So betrayals and disappointments from others follow you. You do not aggressively supervise and critique others who depend on you for that insight. If it is **too weak**, you can be influenced by fame and recognition. You underestimate the personal interests of others. You can believe your marketers and public and, out of a positive mind, stop short of the final purpose you aim toward.*

Synchronization Meditation

Sphinx Kriya

Put your body into cow pose—on the hands and knees with the back gently arched down. Bend the elbows until the forearms come onto the ground. Bring the forearms together. Place both palms flat on the floor with the sides of the thumbs touching. Raise the head slightly. Look at the tip of the nose. Inhale deeply and chant the mantra out loud 8 times as you exhale:

Sat naam sat naam sat naam sat naam
Sat naam sat naam wha-hay gu-roo

Continue for 31 minutes. Then inhale, hold the breath, and concentrate at the brow. Relax at least 1-1/2 hours and have water available to drink when finished. This kriya gives the power to know the past, present, and future. It opens the intuition and gives your words great power and impact on others.

Neutral Mind x Buddhi

Qualities: *When **balanced** the teacher is impersonally personal. It starts with absolute awareness and a neutral assessment from that awareness. It uses intuition to know directly what is real and what is a diversion. Neutral Mind means you respond beyond the positives and negatives. Buddhi Mind means you are clear about the purpose and the laws of each action. A complete Teacher is not an instructor. The Teacher is the expression of Infinity for the benefit of all. You master non-attachment so you are simultaneously in all your activities and not of them. The Teacher Aspect acts on all the other Aspects like a mirror to reveal their true nature and add corrections; you act as a human being not just a human doing. **Too strong,** and you risk a spiritual ego that is attached to the ability to detach and to be "above" normal struggles. **Too weak,** and you can misuse your spiritual and teaching position for personal advantage.*

Core Alignment Meditation

Sodarshan Chakra Kriya

*Sit in easy pose. Eyes are fixed at the tip of the nose. Block the right nostril with the right thumb. Inhale deeply through the left nostril and suspend the breath. Mentally recite the mantra **Wha-hay gu-roo** 16 times while pumping the navel. Pump 3 times with each repetition of the mantra: once on **Wha**, once on **Hay**, and once on **Guroo**, for a total of 48 unbroken pumps.*

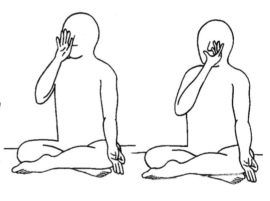

After the 16 repetitions, block the left nostril with the index finger or pinkie and exhale through the right nostril.

Continue for 11 to 31 minutes. Master practitioners may extend this practice to 2-1/2 hours a day.

This kriya has considerable transformational powers. The personal identity is rebuilt, giving the individual a new perspective on the Self. It retrains the mind so that it becomes more user-friendly.

"Intuitive Assessment of Personality Defects to Be Covered"

Neutral Mind x Buddhi/Negative

The best educator knows the weaknesses that must be recognized and compensated for in each student. Every subject has its own requirements that the student needs to match. When the subject is the Self, then the defects are often in the ego or the habits. When refined and **balanced**, this Projection alerts the mind to the habits and patterns that limit you when you want to respond to your insight and understanding of who you are and what to do. You can give effective and precise directives that help your students and colleagues develop their potential. If it is **too strong**, you can become darkly cynical or feel you do not belong with the people who are in your group or family. You have an insight that you know to be true, but feel it will not be accepted or understood by those to whom it matters. If it is **too weak**, you act only as an instructor. You convey knowledge but lack the chisel that chips away the limitations in the student's mind.

Synchronization Meditation

Tantric Kriya

Sit straight. Lift the chest slightly. Raise both hands in front of the chest at the level of the heart center. Place both palms facing upward. Interlace the fingers so they look like slightly curved swords pointing up and outward at 45 degrees. The thumbs are relaxed but point forward. Focus the eyes downward past the nose. Take a breath and chant:

Wha-hay gu-roo wha-hay gu-roo wha-hay gu-roo wha-hay gu-roo

Wha-hay gu-roo wha-hay gu-roo wha-hay gu-roo wha-hay gu-roo

Wha-hay gu-roo wha-hay gu-roo wha-hay gu-roo wha-hay gu-roo

Wha-hay gu-roo wha-hay gu-roo wha-hay gu-roo wha-hay gu-roo

Inhale (about 4 seconds), and chant (about 12 seconds).

Continue for 11 to 31 minutes.

"Interpretations of All Facets of Life"

Neutral Mind x Buddhi/Positive

This Projection has an amazing capacity to take in large amounts of information and sensory impressions. It is active. It develops skills and abilities quickly. It is especially good at understanding the relationships between many parts of a complex system or environment. It cultivates understanding like a web in many directions, all of which connect to a central purpose or area. When **balanced,** *you become an expert in training and development in any area you apply yourself.* **Too much,** *and you can rely on formulas to reach areas that are inherently ineffable. You classify the unnameable.* **Too little,** *and you accumulate knowledge without the depth given by experience.*

Synchronization Meditation

Tershula Kriya

Sit in easy pose. Bring the elbows next to the ribs, forearms extended in front of you, with the hands in front of the heart, right over left, palms up. The hands are approximately 10 degrees higher than the elbows. There is no bend in the wrists. The arms from the fingertips to the elbows form a straight line. The thumbs are extended out to the sides of the hands, the fingertips and palms are slightly offset. The eyes are closed looking at the back of the eyelids. Inhale through the nostrils, pull back on the navel, and suspend the breath. Mentally chant the mantra:

Har har wha-hay gu-roo

for as long as you are able while retaining the breath. While chanting, visualize your hands surrounded by white light. Exhale through the nostrils and visualize lightning shooting out from your fingertips. When you have completely exhaled, hold the breath out, pull Mul Bandh, and again mentally recite the mantra as long as you are able. Inhale deep and continue.

Recommended time of practice is 62 minutes.

This kriya can heal everything. Many psychological disorders or imbalances in the personality can be cured through its practice, and it is helpful in getting rid of phobias, especially father phobia.

"Assessment of Personality Overlords & Their Projections to Be Controlled"

Neutral Mind x Buddhi/Neutral

This is the most mystical and masterful of all the Projections. It gives you depth, dimension, and sensitivity, so you can know exactly how to satisfy that higher consciousness or power you serve. For the self that is the soul; for the saint it is God; and for a worker it is the boss. If you satisfy those essential personality components of the overlord, that lord is obligated to cover the servant or devotee. In the spiritual world it is said that the devotee can undo by prayer what God has written, but God cannot break the knot tied by the compassion and sacrifice of the devotee. The procedure to accomplish this is sadhana, aradhana, and prabupati: discipline, inner attitude, and aptitude, and mastery of God. The distinction between you and God, the devotee and the master, is dissolved. Merger and love is the language and the power of this Projection. Weak and strong do not apply.

Synchronization Meditation

Sit in easy pose, spine straight. Arms stretched out in front, parallel to the ground; palms are facing up with right hand resting in left palm. Begin to chant the Mul Mantra:

**Ek ong kaar, sat naam, kartaa purakh, nirbhao, nirvair
Akaal moorat, ajoonee, saibhang, gurprasaad. Jap.
Aad sach, jugaad sach, haibhee sach, naanak hosee bhee sach**

One Creator and Creation, Truth Identified, Doer of everything, Fearless, Revengeless,
Undying, Unborn, Self-illumined, Guru's Grace. Chant.
True in the beginning, True throughout the ages,
True even now, Nanak says Truth shall ever be.

Hold the posture and chant the mantra 11 times. On the 12th repetition raise the hands over the head, arms straight, and the palms pressed together. Then return to the original position and continue the cycle of 11 repetitions with the arms out straight and 1 repetition with the arms stretched up over the head.

Continue for 11 to 31 minutes.

Resources

This and other KRI products are available from the Kundalini Research Institute (KRI):
www.kriteachings.org.

For information regarding international events: **www.3HO.org**.

To find a teacher in your area or for more information about becoming a Kundalini Yoga teacher:
www.kundaliniyoga.com

Of further interest: **www.sikhnet.org**.

Glossary

Age of Awareness: Another appellative for the Aquarian Age *(see Aquarian Age)*.

Aquarian Age: The next in a succession of astrological ages each lasting roughly 2,000 years. Fully inaugurated in AD 2012, the Aquarian Age will witness a radical change in consciousness, human sensitivity, and technology. The central change of this new age emphasizes an increased sensitivity and evolution of our power of awareness and a new relationship to our mind.

Ahangkar: The transcendental ego, the fundamental principle active in nature and mind that creates boundaries, identity, and attachment to things. It creates the sense of "Me and Mine" which is considered a fundamental tendency in the evolution of complexity and differentiation of objects and thoughts in the universe.

Amrit Vela: Literally "ambrosial time." It is the 2-1/2 hours before the rise of the sun. During this special time you are most receptive to the soul; you can clear the subconscious of wrong habits and impulses; and you can connect with the teachers and saints from all traditions. It is the best time to perform *sadhana* (spiritual discipline).

Antar, Bantar, Jantar, Mantar, Tantar, Patantar, and Sotantar: These describe the sequence of creative expression from inner essence to full manifestation. *Antar* is the inner essence and being. It is before form. Each essence has an associated structure in time and space, a dimension to it, *bantar*. This structure is fulfilled by an appropriate matching set of qualities, *jantar*, which has a unique sound resonance, *mantar*, and a distinct visual form, *yantar*. This form and energy interrelate to the universe, *tantar*, creating a projection and track as it threads through time and space, *patantar*, until finally achieving its liberated form, beyond time and space, *sotantar*. This form creates a neutral point that ties together many of the polarities inherent in *Prakirti* to embed and express the essence of the *antar* in creation.

Applied Mind: A cultivated capacity of the mind which allows you to focus and respond effectively with intuition, intelligence, and comprehensive comparative consciousness to any demand in the environment or toward your goal. It is creative, stress-free, and can act or not act as needed.

Arcline: One of 10 bodies or containing vehicles of a human being. It is a shiny thin arc that goes from ear to ear over the forehead near the normal hairline. It reflects the interaction of the soul of the person with its vital energy resources, and in it are written the potential, destiny, and health of the person.

Aspects: The nine mental patterns formed by the interaction of the three Functional Minds (Negative, Positive, and Neutral) with the three Impersonal Minds (*buddhi, ahangkar,* and *manas*). In the personality they act like fundamental persona or patterns that you use to engage the world.

Atma: The soul or finite form of the Infinite in consciousness. It is transcendental in nature, not a product of the mind but a part of pure awareness. It is a witness of everything and can only be revealed through itself.

Aura: The radiant field of energy and consciousness that surrounds the physical body and which holds and organizes the seven centers of energy called chakras. Its strength, measured by brightness and radius, determines the vitality, mental concerns, and psychophysical integrity of a person.

Awareness: The pure nature of existence; the power to be consciously conscious without an object or need. A fundamental property of the soul and true self; it is Kundalini as it folds and unfolds itself in existence.

Bana: A specified clothing that projects a consciousness.

Bantar: See *Antar.*

Bhagat: A devotee of God.

Breath of Fire: Also called *agni praan.* It is a rapid, rhythmical breath pattern, generated from the navel point and diaphragm with an equal inhale and exhale and usually done through the nose. It is both stimulating and relaxing. It heals, strengthens the nerves, and clears out old patterns and toxins.

Buddhi: This is the first, most etheric manifestation of the Universal Mind from which all other areas of mind are derived. Its quality or function is to give the clarity, discernment, and wisdom that recognize the real from the imaginary. It forms the deepest core of the human psyche but is impersonal, existing independent of the individual sense of self.

Chakra: The word connotes a wheel in action. It usually refers to the seven primary energy centers in the aura that align along the spine from its base to the top of the skull. Each chakra is a center of consciousness with a set of values, concerns, and powers of action associated with it.

Chitta: The mind that permeates all that exists in nature, Universal Mind. It is part of *Prakirti,* transcendental nature. It is not a single state of consciousness but rather the conditions and material that allow consciousness and experience through the senses. *(See also: Universal Mind.)*

Consciousness: The nature of the self and being. In the realm of nature, awareness becomes consciousness. It is from the being itself. Being is expressed in consciousness through contrasts and sensations, in awareness through merger, clarity, and reality.

Core Alignment Meditation: A specific meditation technique used to balance and adjust a particular Aspect of the mind. It facilitates an alignment of the Aspect with the central purpose and flow of the self.

Dharma: A path of righteous living. It is both an ideal of virtue and a path of action that is infused with clear awareness and comprised of actions that are the soul in total synchrony with the universe. It is action without reaction or karma.

Dhyan: *See Meditation.*

Facet: An automatic subconscious predisposition of the mind to act or to prepare to act in a particular way. There are 81 Facets that result from the 27 Projections of the mind interacting with the three Functional Minds. These habits of action can either support your intention and awareness or cloak your consciousness.

Functional Minds: The three minds (Negative, Positive, and Neutral) that act as guides for the personal sense of self.

Gian Mudra: A common hand position used in exercise and meditation, is formed by touching the tip of the index finger to the tip of the thumb. Its effect is receptivity, balance, and gentle expansion.

Golden Chain of Teachers or Golden Link: Historically it is the long line of spiritual masters who have preceded us. Practically it is the subtle link between the consciousness of a student and the master, which has the power to guide and protect the energy of a teaching and its techniques. This link requires the student to put aside the ego and limitations and act in complete synchrony or devotion to the highest consciousness of the master and teachings.

Greater Mind: This is the interconnected network of all minds. The Greater Mind has the ability to sense individual prayer and respond. This is the basis of the power of mental projection to create actions and impact beyond the limits of your own thoughts and concepts.

Gunas: The three qualities or threads that make up the fundamental forces in nature and the mind. Their interactions give motion to the world, stir the larger Greater Mind, and make up the realm of our experience. They are considered inseparable and occur in unlimited combinations. They are abstract; you can only see their effects. They are the *sattva guna* for clarity and purity; the *rajasic guna* for action and transformation, and the *tamasic guna* for heaviness, solidity, and ignorance.

Guru: That which takes us from ignorance to knowledge; from darkness, *gu*, to light, *ru*. It can be a person, a teaching, or in its most subtle form—the Word.

Humanology: A complete system of psychology to promote human excellence and spirit. It incorporates the technology of Kundalini Yoga and meditation, the use of the *Shabd Guru*, and the principles of spiritual counseling.

Ida: One of the three major channels *(nadis)* for subtle energy in the body. It is associated with the flow of breath through the left nostril and represents the qualities of the moon—calmness, receptivity, coolness, and imagination. It is associated with the functions of the parasympathetic nervous system but is not identical to it nor derived from it.

Impersonal Minds: The three major functions of the Universal Mind that create qualities of experience, cognition, and judgment. They are *buddhi, ahangkar,* and *manas.* They are impersonal since they exist independent of or before the individual sense of self.

Intellect: The function of the Universal Mind that releases thoughts, like the churning of the waves on the ocean. It is not the analytical acts of reason. Instead it is the source of the constant stream of thought formation from all levels of the Universal Mind. In this sense, someone who is intellectual is immersed in and often attached to thoughts and the act of making categories.

Intelligence: The use of the mind to create actions that manifest your purpose and the projection of your soul.

Jantar: *See antar.*

Japji Sahib: A mantra, poem, and inspired religious scripture composed by Guru Nanak. *Japji Sahib* gives a view of the cosmos, the soul, the mind, the challenge of life, and the impact of our actions. Its 40 stanzas are a source of many mantras and can be used as a whole or in part to guide both your mind and your heart.

Jappa: Literally "to repeat." It is the conscious, alert, and precise repetition of a mantra.

Kaam: Desire. It connotes the feeling of pleasure and enjoyment of objects and/or feelings. It often implies a sensual or sexual quality. It is one of the five primary blocks to spiritual development.

Kaamanaa: The desire for higher values such as desirelessness, fearlessness, humility, or kindness. One way to deal with the ill-impact of *kaam* is to transform it into *kaamanaa*. Instead of fighting a desire, turn it into the desire for something higher. If you feel greed, be greedy for excellence and humility.

Karma: The law of cause and effect applied to mental, moral, and physical actions. Ego attaches us to and identifies us with objects, feelings, and thoughts. These attachments create a bias toward certain lines of action. Instead of acting you begin reacting. Karmas are the conditions required in order to balance or complete these tendencies. Though necessary, karma is not dictatorial or fatalistic. It is the mechanism that allows the finite experience of existence to maintain and stabilize itself. We all have free will and can take actions to re-direct the momentum of a karma. We can transform it or neutralize it using meditation, *jappa*, good deeds, or intuition that remove your sense of ego and the identification with that past line of action.

Karta Purkh: *See maya and Purkha.*

Kriya: Literal meaning is "completed action." A Kundalini Yoga Kriya is a sequence of postures and yoga techniques used to produce a particular impact on the psyche, body, or self. The structure of each *kriya* has been designed to generate, organize, and deliver a particular state or change of state, thereby completing a cycle of effect. These effects have been codified and elaborated by Yogi Bhajan and form the basic tools used in yoga and its therapeutic applications.

Krodh: Anger. It connotes the negative parts of the experience of anger. Unreleased internal anger leads to confusion and impulsive action. This results in a loss of the inner clarity, wisdom, and sense of guidance derived from *buddhi*.

Kundalini Yoga: It is a Raaj Yoga that creates vitality in the body, balance in the mind, and openness to the spirit. It is used by the householder, busy in the world, to create immediate clarity. The fourth Guru in the Sikh tradition, Guru Ram Das, was acknowledged as the greatest Raaj Yogi. *(See Raaj Yogi.)* He opened this long secret tradition to all.

Lobh: Greed. The quality of always grasping and feeling your self through what you have or what you consume. It is a principal block to clear consciousness and the spirit. It is diminished through the practice of non-attachment, contentment, and self-sacrifice.

Mahan Tantric: A Master of White Tantric Yoga. This title and function was bestowed upon Yogi Bhajan in 1971. There is only one Mahan Tantric alive on the earth at any one time.

Manas: The lower or sensory mind. It is one of the three impersonal functions of the Universal Mind. It deals with sensory impressions, sequences, and the desires and impulses generated from their combinations. It is the closest to what traditional western psychology deals with as the mind.

Mantar: *See mantra and antar.*

Mantra: Sounds or words that tune or control the mind. *Man* means mind. *Tra-ng* is the wave or movement of the mind. Mantra is a wave, a repetition of sound and rhythm that directs or controls the mind. When you recite a mantra you have impact: through the meridian points in the mouth, through its meaning, through its pattern of energy, through its rhythm, and through its *naad*—energetic shape in time. Recited correctly a mantra will activate areas of the nervous system and brain and allow you to shift your state and the perceptual vision or energetic ability associated with it.

Maya: The creative power of the Creator that restricts and limits. It creates the sense of limitation that leads us to identify with experience, the ego, and things. Because of this it is often thought of as the illusion that blocks us from the spirit. But, as Guru Nanak (see Sikh Gurus) reminds us, you need not be attached to the productions of *maya*. Instead they can be used to serve and express the higher consciousness and spirit. *Maya* is simply *Karta Purkh*, the doing of the Great Being. *Maya* takes the ineffable into the realm of the measurable.

Meditation: *Dhyan.* It is a process of deep concentration or merger into an object or a state of consciousness. Meditation releases reactions and unconscious habits and build the spontaneous and intuitive link to awareness itself.

Moh: Delusion and attachment.

Mudra: Mudra means "seal." It usually refers to hand positions used in meditation and exercise practices. These hand positions are used to seal the body's energy flow in a particular pattern. More generally it can refer to other locks, *bandhas* (see *Mul Bandh*), and meditation practices that seal the flow of energy by concentration.

Mul Bandh: This literally means "root lock." It is a body lock used to balance *prana* and *apana* (see *prana*) at the navel point. This releases reserve energy which is used to arouse the Kundalini. It is a contraction of the lower pelvis—the navel point, the sex organs, and the rectum.

Naad: The inner sound that is subtle and all-present. It is the direct expression of the Absolute. Meditated upon, it leads into a sound current that pulls the consciousness into expansion.

Naam: The manifested identity of the essence. The word derives from *Naa-ay-ma , which* means "that which is not, now is born." A *Naam* gives identity, form, and expression to that which was only essence or subtle before. It is also referred to as the Word.

Naam Simran: This refers to the state and act of deep meditation by dwelling and merging into the names of the Infinite, of God.

Nadi: Channels or pathways of subtle energy. It is said that there are over 72,000 primary ones throughout the body.

Navel Point: The sensitive area of the body near the umbilicus that accumulates and stores life force. It is the reserve energy from this area that initiates the flow of the Kundalini energy from the base of the spine. If the navel area is strong, your vital force and health are also strong.

Negative Mind: One of the three Functional Minds. It is the fastest and acts to defend you. It asks, "How can this harm me? How can this limit or stop me?" It is also the power to just say no, stop something, or reject a direction of action.

Neutral Mind: The most refined and often the least developed of the three Functional Minds. It judges and assesses. It witnesses and gives you clarity. It holds the power of intuition and the ability to see your purpose and destiny. It is the gateway for awareness.

Patantar: See Antar.

Pavan Guru: Literally, the "breath of the guru." It is the transformative wisdom that is embedded in the patterns of breath, especially those patterns generated in the expression of *naad* in sound or mantra.

Pingala: One of the three major channels *(nadis)* for subtle energy in the body. It is associated with the flow of breath through the right nostril and represented the qualities of the sun—energy, heat, action, and projective power. It is associated with the functions of the sympathetic nervous system but is not identical to it or derived from it.

Positive Mind: One of the three Functional Minds. It elaborates, magnifies, extends, and assists. It asks, "How can this help me? How can I use this? What is the positive side of this?"

Prakirti: Transcendental Nature. It is creation as we can experience it. It includes mind and matter. It is formed from the motion and interaction of the *gunas*. It is multi-leveled and evolved from the original consciousness of the Absolute.

Prana: The universal life force that gives motion. It is the breath in air. It is the subtle breath of the *purusha* as it vibrates with a psychophysical energy or presence. *Prana* regulates the modes and moods of the mind.

Pranayam: Regulated breathing patterns or exercises.

Pratyahaar: One of the eight limbs of yoga, it is the synchronization of the thoughts with the Infinite. To quote Yogi Bhajan; "*Pratyahaar* is the control of the mind through withdrawal of the senses. The joy in your life, which you really want to enjoy, is within you. There is nothing more precise than you within you. The day you find the you within you, your mind will be yours. In *pratyahaar* we bring everything to zero *(shuniaa)*, as *pranayam* brings everything to Infinity."

Projection: A stance of the psyche projecting into action. It is an attitude of your mind that is a tendency to approach action in a certain way. There are 27 Projections that arise from the nine Aspects of the mind interacting with the three Functional Minds.

Purkha: The great Being of existence.

Purusha: The transcendental self, soul, *atma,* or spirit. It is the first contained embodiment of the unlimited consciousness and is formed with the subtle body. It is the consciousness and witness of the spirit that indwells the body.

Raaj Yogi: A yogi who follows the royal or highest path. One who excels and exalts the self in the midst of life without monastic withdrawal. One who places the self on the throne and presides with consciousness over all domains of manifestation, internal and external. *(See Kundalini Yoga, Yogi.)*

Sadhana: A spiritual discipline; the early morning practice of yoga, meditation, and other spiritual exercises.

Saa-Taa-Naa-Maa: This is referred to as the Punj Shabd Mantra (*panj* means five). It is the "atomic" or *naad* form of the mantra *Sat Naam.* It is used to increase intuition, balance the hemispheres of the brain, and to create a destiny for someone when there was none.

Sat: Existence; what is; the subtle essence of Infinity itself.

Sat Naam: The essence or seed embodied in form; the identity of truth. When used as a greeting it means "I greet and salute that reality and truth which is your soul." It is called the Bij Mantra—the seed for all that comes.

Sattvic: One of the three basic qualities of nature *(gunas).* It represents purity, clarity, and light.

Shabd: Sound, especially subtle sound or sound imbued with consciousness. It is a property or emanation of consciousness itself. If you meditate on *shabd* it awakens your awareness.

Shabd Guru: These are sounds spoken by the Gurus; the vibration of the Infinite Being which transforms your consciousness; the sounds and words captured by the Gurus in the writings which comprise the *Siri Guru Granth Sahib.*

Shakti: The creative power and principle of existence itself. Without it nothing can manifest or bloom. It is feminine in nature.

Shuniaa: A state of the mind and consciousness where the ego is brought to zero or complete stillness. There a power exists. It is the fundamental power of a Kundalini Yoga teacher. When you become *shuniaa* then the One will carry you. You do not grasp or act. With folded hands you "are not." It is then that Nature acts for you.

Shushmanaa: One of the three major channels *(nadis)* for subtle energy in the body. It is associated with the central channel of the spine and is the place of neutrality through which the Kundalini travels when awakened. When mantra is vibrated from this place it has the power of soul and consciousness.

Sikh Gurus: In the Sikh tradition there were 10 living Gurus and one Guru, the *Shabd Guru*—the Word that guided and flowed through each of them. This succession of 10 Gurus revealed the Sikh path over a 200-year period. They were:

1st Sikh Guru: Guru Nanak	6th Sikh Guru: Guru Hargobind
2nd Sikh Guru: Guru Angad	7th Sikh Guru: Guru Har Rai
3rd Sikh Guru: Guru Amar Das	8th Sikh Guru: Guru Har Krishan
4th Sikh Guru: Guru Ram Das	9th Sikh Guru: Guru Teg Bahadur
5th Sikh Guru: Guru Arjan	10th Sikh Guru: Guru Gobind Singh

The 10th Sikh Guru, Guru Gobind Singh, passed the Guruship to the *Siri Guru Granth Sahib,* which embodies the writings, teachings, and sound current of the Gurus.

Simran: A deep meditative process in which the *naam* of the Infinite is remembered and dwelled in without conscious effort.

Siri Guru Granth Sahib: Sacred compilation of the words of the Sikh Gurus as well as of Hindu, Muslim, Sufi, and other saints. It captures the expression of consciousness and truth derived when in a state of divine union with God. It is written in *naad* and embodies the transformative power and structure of consciousness in its most spiritual and powerful clarity. It is a source of many mantras.

Sotantar: *See antar.*

Subtle Body: *See Ten Bodies.*

Synchronization Meditation: A meditation used to balance or develop one of the 27 Projections of the mind. It synchronizes the Projection to support the associated Aspect in action.

Tamas: One of the three basic qualities of nature *(gunas)*. It represents heaviness, slowness, and dullness. It is inertia and confusion.

Tantar: *See Antar.*

Tattvas: A category of cosmic existence; a stage of reality or being; a "thatness" of differentiated qualities. In total there are 36 *tattvas*. Each wave of differentiation has its own rules and structure. The final five tattvas are called the gross elements and have the phasic qualities and relationships of ether, air, fire, water, and earth.

Ten Bodies: We are all spiritual beings having a human experience. In order to have this experience the spirit takes on 10 bodies or vehicles. They are the Soul Body, the three Mental Bodies (Negative, Positive, and Neutral Minds), the Physical Body, Pranic Body, Arcline Body, Auric Body, Subtle Body, and Radiant Body. Each body has its own quality, function, and realm of action.

Third Eye Point: The sixth chakra or center of consciousness. It is located at a point on the forehead between the eyebrows. Associated with the functioning of the pituitary gland, it is the command center and integrates the parts of the personality. It gives you insight, intuition, and the understanding of meanings and impacts beyond the surface of things. For this reason it is the focal point in many meditations.

Universal Mind: This refers to the entire spectrum of mental existence and sentient potential in the universe in whatever form. Mind and matter are considered gradations of transcendental nature, *Prakirti,* and can exist without or before a particular entity to experience it. *(See also chitta.)*

Wahe Guru: A mantra of ecstasy and dwelling in God. It is the Infinite teacher of the soul. Also called the *gur mantra.*

Yogi: One who has attained a state of yoga (union) where polarities are mastered and transcended. One who practices the disciplines of yoga and has attained self-mastery.

Index